E

Publishing

1

Watch for More Titles
from Dianne Hobbs

and *Empower Publishing*

LOSING MY MIND

A LONELY JOURNEY

BY

DIANNE HOBBS

Empower Publishing
Winston-Salem

Empower

Publishing

Empower Publishing
PO Box 26701
Winston-Salem, NC 27114

The opinions expressed in this work are entirely the opinions of the author and do not represent the opinions or thoughts of the publisher. The author has represented and warranted all ownership and/or legal right to publish all the materials in this book.

First Empower Publishing Books edition published January, 2022
Empower Publishing, Feather Pen, and all production design are trademarks.

For information regarding bulk purchases of this book, digital purchase and special discounts, please contact the publisher at publish.empower.now@gmail.com

Cover art by Dianne Hobbs

Manufactured in the United States of America
ISBN 978-1-63066-528-9

This book is dedicated to my son Andrew, who took time out from his life to save mine.

—Dianne Hobbs

Acknowledgments

When the pandemic began my dear sister-in-law and lifelong friend, Thomasina Ring, encouraged me to write this story. She's an editor and author, and we laugh together at my mistakes, typos, wandering story line and unnecessary elaborations (TMI she reminded me. "Too much information."). She's always been my "soul mate." She's spent countless hours correcting my grammar and typing mistakes and rewording my often-confusing sentences. She has kept me to the "story arc" and is the source of much of what is good about the book. Any further mistakes are mine! I thank her and love her with all my heart! "Thank you," she says, blushing.

A huge debt of gratitude goes to my zoom writing group, led by Susan Surman, renowned author, playwright, and actor. Susan has been unstinting in offering her time and advice. Without her and the group I would not have finished this book. I needed the group's supportive space and insight to find the strength to continue writing in my own voice. I owe you more gratitude than I can express. And I look forward to continuing our meetings in the future. Your feedback is invaluable. Your talents inspire me!

I've been through countless drafts, and it's one of the most rewarding things I've ever done. I love writing more than just about anything I've done in my life. The time flies by, and I have to set alarms to remember to eat and feed my new cat!

I thank Andrew and Larisa for interrupting their lives out of love for me. I owe them a debt I can never repay. Without them, I wouldn't be here and wouldn't have improved as I did. I thank them for their support and their unwavering faith in me and especially for their patience and forgiveness at stressful times during my long journey to wellness. I thank them for making it possible for me to live independently and happily in my home. And thanks to them for staying nearby for support. And now they have been blessed with the birth of their first child, a son!

I wish to thank my brothers, David, John, and Jim, and my sister Elizabeth, and their spouses Leigh, Diane and Elaine for their support, help, and assistance. I don't know where I would be today without their love, laughter and songs! Thank you to my niece Jean for her encouragement and advice on finishing my book! And I'm grateful to my half-brother Robert for his several readings of my manuscript, his helpful comments and sorely needed computer help.

Many thanks to my church folk, my dear friend from my youth, Skinner, my supportive group of "gurls," and the art teachers who enriched my life. A special thanks and recognition goes to Shepherd's Center programs and to Trans-Aid services provided for the elderly in my town of Piedmont, North Carolina.

And thanks from my heart to the many therapists who taught me how to move and think again.

This book is the result of many who contributed. I have changed my views of medicine, especially for the elderly because of my experiences.

And importantly, I would like to thank my publisher Mike Simpson, Empower Publishing, for all his hard work in getting my book draft into print. I couldn't have asked for a better person to work with. He was unfailingly encouraging and patient with me as he led me through this process. Kudos to him with gratitude! I look forward to working together in the future.

Forward

Over my lifetime I have been a folk singer, an employment counselor, a bank teller, an administrative assistant, a security officer, both high school and college counselors, a learning resources coordinator for medical personnel, a vice president for personnel and training of a large national insurance company, and have installed computer medical systems in a seven state region. I became a healthy first-time mother at the age of forty-four.

But I was never diagnosed with Alzheimer's Disease. Until three years ago.

This is my story.

Names of medical staff and facilities have been changed.

Chapter One: A Bad Fall

Early on a pleasant sunny spring morning in 2017, I went for a jog in a large park two blocks down the hill from my house in Piedmont, North Carolina. As I ran down the street and into the park, I noticed the trees were filling out with green leaves, leaving the trails shaded. Jogging down the trail I passed the baseball diamond to my left where spring training for the nearby high school had started. I could see and hear faintly the coaches exhorting the players to greater efforts. Otherwise the park was deserted and peaceful. I was happy, the temperature was cool, and all was perfect for a morning run.

How good it felt to be jogging effortlessly at seventy-three years of age! I had always led a fit and active life. I wished that my partner was with me. But he was back home. Asleep. I sighed, longing for him not to be so sedentary. He never walked or ran with me. My expectations of him had been different. He had told me that he enjoyed running. Not so, I discovered. Oh well, it's not imperative that we have the same likes and dislikes, I thought philosophically. Different interests can keep our relationship alive.

I continued down the smooth dirt path, looking over to the high school running track and the tennis courts. When I came to steps leading to a path toward home, I began jogging down them. In the blink of an eye, I was horrified to see that the concrete steps were broken, and I was going to fall! Instantly I decided to fall over a 12-inch wall to my left because I saw there was a pile of jagged broken steps on the right. The best of two bad choices! Too late I noticed that a large broken piece of concrete, like a paving stone, was hidden beside the left wall in tall grass. I wanted to pause in mid-air. This was really going to hurt! I resigned myself to it. As I pitched over the wall, I braced myself with my hands, but was unable to stop myself from hitting the concrete. Chin first. I heard my brain go "thunk" against the front of my skull. Then everything went blank.

I came to after an unknown period of time and looked around dazed and confused. I lay on the concrete and raised my head a little. Then I did nothing. After checking my body for broken bones, I gingerly pushed myself to a sitting position, realizing I could move. Not knowing how long I had been unconscious, I looked around me. I was frightened and didn't know what to do next. I wasn't even sure where I was.

I felt no pain. Good. Maybe I hadn't hurt myself. But I was woozy and felt weak. From the far end of the park, I could hear noises from the baseball team I had seen earlier but knew I couldn't make it that far to get their attention. I became more and more frightened. I kept thinking I would stay out on the ground forever. I would never be able to make it back home. No one would ever find me. I might die alone on what was turning out not to be a wonderful day in the park. I was actually beginning to panic.

I could see through chain link fences surrounding tennis courts. Alongside them a woman was jogging perpendicular to me far down the park past the courts. I saw we would intercept at a bridge not far in front of me. I knew I had to move toward the bridge and get her attention.

I slowly and carefully pushed myself to a crouching, then standing position, checking out my body every inch of the way. Swaying slightly, feeling shaky, testing a step, then two, I started down the path toward the bridge. When she was closer, I called out to her loudly, "*Hello*"! Thank God she looked over and saw me. She hurried to where I was standing.

She looked upset (well, horrified) and asked, "Are you okay?" I looked down and saw blood had dripped from my face and hands all over my shirtfront. This was the first time I had noticed it. I still felt no pain so the blood didn't frighten me.

I replied, "I want to wash myself off at the water fountain," which was right in front of me.

In retrospect, I have no idea why that was the first thing I thought to say. I remember being oddly embarrassed at my predicament. And as a woman who grew up in the south, I couldn't imagine walking around looking the way I did. Again, it didn't occur to me to think I might be seriously injured.

She walked over to the water fountain and told me her name was Millicent. "I'm Dianne," I replied.

"How can I help you?" she asked, looking more worried than I felt. I remember being extremely grateful that I was no longer alone. Haltingly I replied, "I fell back there on those steps. Could you by any chance drive me home? It's up a steep hill, and I don't think I can make it by myself."

She said her car was in a parking lot a few blocks away but she would go for it, drive back, and get me. She helped me walk up to the street, leaving me at a safe corner where I could lean against a stop sign. She asked if I could stand for a little while and I nodded. "Yes I think so. Thank you so much."

She quickly ran away. Somehow I knew I could trust her to return. She was about forty, strong and fit, with the wiry body of a runner. She had a compassionate demeanor.

I now know her car was up a big hill and at least five blocks away. She didn't even mention that to me.

Chapter Two: My Good Samaritan

I watched her, not thinking about anything but how to keep standing up to wait until she returned. I held onto the stop sign with a death grip using both my hands, afraid I would fall again. I was at a three-way stop.

After a few minutes, I noticed people dressed for work were staring at me from their car windows, not ten feet away, as I stood there, blood running down my face and covering my shirt, and now arms and legs. *No one said a thing to me.* They just stared blankly. Their indifference to me is imprinted indelibly upon my mind. Again, thank God for Millicent and her willingness to go out of her way to help me.

I now think of the many people who heard a female jogger screaming for help as she was being attacked in New York's Central Park. Later people said they heard her but didn't want to get involved. I guess the people who looked my way that morning felt the same way. They might be late for work.

Millicent returned soon and helped me into her car. I directed her to my home two blocks up the steep hill and around a corner, then two blocks down another hill. We reached my house on the right side of the street. As she parked in front of the daunting three-story granite steps leading up to my house, she looked up at them and said calmly, "I'll help you up to your front porch."

She looked over at my right hand holding on to her door handle and said, "Your hand looks like you might have broken it." I hadn't felt it, but now I looked and was surprised at how swollen it was. My first two knuckles were bloody and standing up about an inch. It didn't hurt. I just observed it. All I could think about was getting up to my front door.

"Is there anyone at home to take care of you?" she asked.

"My partner Jude is here, but he's probably still asleep." He slept until after ten every day.

She held securely on to my arm and helped me slowly and carefully up the steps. We finally reached my front porch, and I rang the doorbell. It's a measure of my state of shock that I didn't think to use my house key, which was in my pocket. It took a number of rings before Jude finally came to the door. In his pajamas.

Millicent introduced herself and said to him, "Dianne fell in the park. I'm a medical professional, and I think she needs to go to the emergency room. She hit her head on concrete, lost consciousness briefly, she thinks, and has probably broken her hand and maybe her chin. She seems a little confused and shaky to me."

He thanked her. She said she worked at the nearby hospital's rehabilitation center and headed up a program designed to help elderly people regain and keep their physical and cognitive functions. She said, "In addition to treating Dianne's visible injuries, her head trauma should be taken seriously, especially when there is loss of consciousness and especially if it occurs to an older person. Effects can manifest later." She recommended we go to the Emergency Room to get a brain scan. She asked us to contact her to let her know how I was doing that day or the next, as she was worried about me.

I sent her a large bouquet of flowers the next day thanking her from the bottom of my heart. Words can't express my gratitude for her kindness and professionalism. I will never forget her. She was there when I needed her and, though we were strangers, she not only drove me home but she calmed me in my confusion and panic.

Chapter Three: A Cursory Home Exam

My partner, Jude McCain, seemed calm and not at all worried or even solicitous. This confused me even further. He seemed like a stranger. His medical doctor persona, I guess. A retired Board-Certified Neurologist, he began examining me, giving me a professional exam. I recognized it as such, because we had been partners for thirteen years, and I was a well-trained amateur neurologist (though without portfolio)! He asked me if I was nauseated, dizzy, woozy, feeling faint, sleepy, was having a headache, leg pain and more questions. He performed some reaction tests on me. He examined my head, my chin, my hand and the cuts on my legs. He tracked my eye movements and looked into the pupils.

"You've bled a lot," he said, "but all injuries on the head do bleed profusely. I see a bump on your chin and a small cut in your mouth. Your knees and legs are skinned and bleeding. Your hand is swollen at the knuckles. What hurts?"

"I'm not hurting anywhere," I replied. I think I was in shock.

"The cut in your mouth is a small cut and will heal on its own." He palpated the bump on my chin but didn't think it was broken. He asked me to move my fingers and hand but didn't think they were broken either.

He then asked me to get up and walk across the room. I felt unsteady on my feet and told him I felt awkward and shaky walking. My legs just didn't feel they were under me. I still wasn't in pain. We weighed the option of going to the ER where he said we would face a long wait before being seen or staying at home where Jude could watch me and decide what to do.

Naturally we decided I would stay with Jude. He had worked in an Emergency Room and knew the protocols there. He thought he could go through the same steps the staff there would.

However, strangely embarrassed, I told him I was worried that maybe I had a subdural hematoma. This question came from my years of watching every TV episode of "Ben Casey, MD." Dr. Casey always seemed to have a patient whom he heroically diagnosed in the nick of time with a subdural hematoma. I got so I could diagnose it before he did! Jude thought seriously, and then courteously said we should watch for that. I appreciated his not making fun of my concern.

He didn't mention the fact that he wouldn't be able to perform any brain or bone scans from home. I now realize I should have had my brain scanned because of my fall and loss of consciousness but it never crossed my mind.

We never did go to the Emergency Room that day or the next or ever, as I was only sore and "shaken up" per Jude. I didn't feel at all like myself but that was vague, and I couldn't express it well enough for it to be a serious symptom to Jude. My injuries were beginning to be painful, but that was expected from the abrasions I had suffered. After a few more days, I was still sore, shaky and spacey but feeling a little better. My cuts and bruises eventually healed, but I continued to have trouble walking. Again, this was not considered serious enough by Jude, and therefore, by me, to see a doctor.

But oh, dear reader, walking was later to become a serious problem. And though unnoticed at the time, my fall in April started a downward spiral in my mind as well.

Chapter Four: My Partner Jude's Mental Health

In 1978 Jude had become Board Certified in Neurology. He had begun his practice in a small town near Piedmont, North Caroline where I lived. Over time he become extremely well-respected and had built up a successful practice. He had even been given a special wing of the hospital to house the large number of patients he was treating. (I explain his background to the reader because of how it later affected my medical decision-making.)

He had been married for 22 years to a woman, Dolores, he had met prior to medical school. I met her when she began working at the high school where I was a counselor, and she immediately began confiding in me almost daily. She told me Jude had built her a lavish house after he had begun his practice. It had a heated pool surrounded by a large patio. It was perfect for entertaining and they did so frequently, having a large circle of friends. She complained that he was "never" home and constantly busy reading journals when he was. She was contemplating a divorce.

Astonished, I told her I understood that it's normal for a busy and successful doctor to work nights and weekends, and many of their wives have trouble with it. No comment from her on my counselor-ey comment. Inwardly, I was thinking she was not a particularly empathetic person. I thought it was churlish of her to complain.

She was sociable and extroverted. She said Jude was a "stick-in-the-mud" who didn't like to party. He did, however, like to drink and have long conversations with his doctor friends to relax. One funny story she told me took place at one of their parties. A doctor asked Jude what his specialty was, and he said, "Neurology." The doctor pulled him over to the side and then pointed downward and said, "Doc, I've been having trouble urinating. Can you help me?" It turned out during the fifteen years of his career, most doctors in town were referring all their elderly patients to him for interpretation of brain scans, treatment of strokes, dementia and brain tumors. Of all the patients he took care of, most were very sick, elderly and dying. He worked long hours and was called frequently to the hospital at night for emergencies. He brought MRI scans home each night to examine and would dictate his medical records from there. Jude didn't want to lose money by hiring staff or other doctors, Dolores told me. This stress and overwork led to a serious nervous breakdown. He was hospitalized and tested. His diagnosis was bipolar disorder (manic-depressive) and overwork. When he was in the manic phase, he would feel the energy to work long hours, make grandiose plans, refuse to turn down patient referrals, was impulsive and had poor judgment about his own needs and physical shape. His depressive moods caused him to withdraw into prolonged silences and become irritable. He was also diagnosed as an alcoholic.

I wondered how he could have improved without his wife's support. She spoke of him with a complete lack of sympathy or understanding. It must have been difficult for her to accept his change in circumstances. She must have been angry. But he was still her husband and deserved some help, I thought.

"He began drinking a lot instead of accepting the recommended treatment," Dolores said. "His colleagues and coworkers tried to help him to no avail. As a consequence of his drinking and erratic behavior over time, he was asked to retire and lost his practice."

How terrible for both of them!

He was forced to go on disability. They had to sell their large home and move to a smaller one back in my home town. This had all come to a head in 1993, just the same year Dolores and I started commuting together.

They were not divorced, but she said she was tired of him sitting in the living room every day, depressed, and doing nothing. He was being treated but did not follow the doctor's

9

instructions, again resorting to self-medicating with drink. Red flag alert for me. He needs help. My help. The counselor and mother in me immediately felt sorry for her but mostly for Jude. He had been at the pinnacle of a successful career. He had made it through the grueling medical training needed to become Board Certified. He had won professional accolades from his colleagues. He then lost his practice, his self-respect, the respect of his former colleagues and of his wife. However, he had a medical diagnosis which I understood. It had been in my family history. I tried to explain what bipolar meant. It was an illness which he could not help. She wasn't interested in what was happening to him.

I thought I could fix him. I felt compassion for him. As Jude later said, "If it moves, you mother it." He meant this as a criticism. However, I took it as a compliment.

I met Jude in Christmas of that same year. Dolores, now divorced from Jude who had moved out of state, asked me if she and her family could celebrate Christmas with my son and me. She said Jude was visiting for the holidays. The doorbell rang, and Dolores walked in with one of the handsomest men I had ever seen. He had intense light blue eyes, dark hair, and was like an old-fashioned gentleman, polite and glad to meet my son Andrew and me. His voice was deep and resonant. He had something to say to each of us in greeting. He made us comfortable as if he were the host.

I looked into his eyes and was mesmerized by him. I couldn't believe this was the man Dolores had described. She must have been exaggerating his condition. In addition, he introduced all their three children who had his blue eyes and were witty and intelligent. Actually, an altogether beautiful family, including Dolores.

I planned to attend the Midnight Service at my church after dinner and asked his family if they would like to go with me. They were tired and had to go home.

I attended church alone full of dreams that had nothing to do with Christmas Eve.

Chapter Five: "Snowed on Him."

Thus began a relationship which later turned out to be the most passionate love affair of my life. Even after that one evening, I thought of Jude frequently. When I was a teenager, I would have said I was "snowed" on him. I daydreamed that someday, somehow we would be together. But I didn't hear from him immediately or even soon.

For the next *eleven years* we corresponded by phone, at first every four to six months. Early on, we had a kind of "virtual" relationship. Once or twice, a year went by without my hearing from him. I later discovered he had suffered periodic episodes of mental illness, mainly depression. He also had periods when he would drink heavily. I wouldn't hear from him during those times. Naturally I didn't experience the full extent of his illness. Strangely, I was patient with these interruptions and even thought they were a good thing. We were taking our time. But I felt connected to him spiritually. Our talks had been extraordinary. He had the ability to get into my head and live there. I respected him regardless of his mental illness. He still had his brilliant intellect. I learned a lot from him. My counseling work improved.

Gradually we began to talk more frequently. Our calls grew to every few weeks, then every week. When he came to visit his children, he would swing by my house, and we would take long walks together. I maintained my strong feelings for him and had no interest in other men. Our relationship manifested itself as good friends. I tamped down my romantic feelings in favor of a warm mutual affection.

Being a psychiatrist in addition to a neurologist, Jude was a great listener, and we talked for hours on the phone. In the spring of 2004, Jude drove south to visit his sons. He stayed with his wife during visits.

Dolores asked me to date him one night when he was

visiting so she could go out with her boyfriend. I agreed. I had grown very close to Jude. We held hands in the movie and talked for hours later over a bottle of Pinot Noir.

We had many dates during his more and more frequent visits to his sons. Dolores said she liked it that we were seeing each other. *OK!*

I, a woman past middle age, began to experience the exalted feeling of being in love. The sun was brighter. I looked forward to going to work each day. I chatted happily with everyone I met. No more was I the introvert I had turned into since my divorce. I was always smiling at everyone and was told I was glowing. Every morning upon awakening I would feel energized. I loved all the students I counseled. It was like being on drugs. It was a delightful time.

We were intensely romantic, choosing and playing romantic music to each other during our calls. Finally Jude made an extended visit to me. During that trip, the two of us went camping at the beach. As we walked beside the waves at sunset, Jude got down on his knees and asked me to marry him. I was totally shocked. I said no! It was far too soon. I was not ready for that step and never planned to marry again.

This might have been the only wise decision I made about Jude.

He then proposed that we live together.

In the spring of 2005, after talking about it a lot, we impulsively decided on trial living arrangements before we permanently began sharing our lives. I spoke to my sixteen-year-old son Andrew about it. He liked Jude. He had no objections. Jude and I immediately began living together in my home in Piedmont, North Carolina. After six months we made the move permanent.

I explained to him again as we made the decision I didn't want to get married. I wanted the type of relationship where we would never take each other for granted. Unknown to him, I had some minor hidden doubts about the wisdom of my decision. His proposal of marriage out of the blue had unsettled me a little. It seemed impulsive. And did mention I was seven years older than he? But I put these doubts aside in favor of all our interactions over the past years. I felt I loved him and could offer the support he needed. It was intensely romantic.

Silly me. *Why did I make this move when I knew his previous problems?*

I was blinded by his background and how handsome, educated and erudite he was. I put him on a pedestal because of his abilities and significant credentials as a physician. He was a Svengali.

He was a DOCTOR! This worshipful attitude toward him continued for quite a while. I actually saw him as a godlike character. This was not fair to him or to me. I now have 20/20 hindsight. I was an accomplished woman. I had been vice president of a large national health insurance company before becoming a counselor after Andrew's birth. I was in love and wasn't using my brain. I was over 60 years old and was facing an empty nest when my son would leave home for college in a few years. I dreaded living alone. I still thought I could love Jude enough to fix him. I was thinking with my heart and, well, other parts of my anatomy. This exaggerated love for and respect toward Jude explains some of my actions to come.

Chapter Six: Living Together

I retired in 2007. The next eight years were, by and large, happy ones. Andrew left for college, Appalachian State in North Carolina. Jude and I adjusted to just the two of us being together in my home. We got along except when Jude's mental illness would crop up. The psychiatrist I insisted he begin seeing had to constantly tweak Jude's meds to keep him on an even keel. He was experiencing manic episodes, hypomania (per his doctor), a state of irritability, restlessness, and general meanness and unpleasantness (my diagnosis). When depressed he sank into silence. This was essentially bipolar illness or manic/depression. He drank to excess at times. His behavior during either situation was unbearable. I had never seen this side of him. Maybe I wasn't the loving and supportive person I had imagined myself to be.

I finally learned to walk away when he became verbally abusive. Otherwise I would end up crying and screaming at him. He knew how to hit my hot buttons. He truly had mental problems, far more serious than I had imagined. And had become harder to live with. He would turn me irritable and mean too, which was not my nature. Of course, afterwards, he and I would be remorseful, and we would both forgive and forget. After all, we would love and support each other through sickness and health, we had vowed. I stubbornly refused to consider separating.

Andrew visited from App State on school holidays and vacations. The years went by. After returning to California to live with his father again, Andrew went back to finish college. He graduated in 2017. He and his fiancee Larisa moved to Oregon where Andrew had obtained employment as a chef.

Jude and I definitely were not as happy as we had been in the beginning. We seemed too often to be on an emotional roller coaster. I could never fully relax, not knowing when he would have some kind of flare-up. Yet I was determined to see it through. I still believed in Jude's innate goodness and still loved him with all my heart. It was just getting harder to live with him.

Chapter Seven: Double Troubles

And then I fell while jogging in the park in the spring of 2017. I had trouble walking. But later as the summer progressed, I had slowly begun to feel more normal. Often I still had trouble with my balance while walking, but I continued working to improve. I seemed at times to be getting better. Dizzy moments and balance problems came and went.

I was beginning to be worried, though, about my inability to walk properly. Jude didn't seem to be interested in discussing it, saying it didn't seem serious to him. So I adopted a wait-and-see attitude.

What happened next made it clearer why Jude was relatively uninterested in my problems. He himself was in pain.

During the summer and early fall of 2017, Jude had to have two hip replacements, separated by a few months. The hospital had many connecting buildings and only one parking lot. The operating and hospital rooms were a long way from that parking facility, and I began to get much worse at walking. I would need to stop several times and sit down on the way to and from his room several times each day. I was walking through a lot of imbalance and pain. It didn't occur to me to ask for some kind of assistance—a walker or a wheelchair. My mind was totally occupied with Jude's problems, and, of course, I didn't want to bring up my personal difficulties at such a terrible time for him. It seemed minor in comparison to his situation. I knew it would be asking too much of him to consider my problems, so I didn't. I took care of him as best I could.

I spent each night in the chair beside him in the hospital, waking every 15 minutes when nurses came in to check, give him meds, or turn off the alarm on the intravenous fluid machine. False alarms happened frequently. I was tempted to take care of them myself after seeing it done umpteen times, but the nurse convinced me that one of those alarms could be the real thing, instead of a faulty sensor. I dropped my plan.

Although hospitals are places where illnesses and injuries are treated with the utmost professionalism, there were moments of hilarity. This was a teaching hospital, meaning unrehearsed "events" might occur now and then.

Once, a Code Blue was called, and a large group of wide-eyed medical personnel galloped down the hall and into the room, dashing over to Jude dragging along with them all kinds of medical equipment and carts. They shouted, "What's wrong?"

"Nothing", said Jude, "but I do have to go to the bathroom."

Just then, another doctor ran into the room and yelled, "Next door!" and they all dashed out of the room dragging their carts and equipment behind them. The Keystone Cops!

One night a cute young nurse entered Jude's room to deliver his medicines. "How are we tonight?" she chirped.

He said, "I'm fine, but the guy in the bed beside me isn't doing so well."

There was no bed or man beside him in his room.

Without blinking, she asked, "Oh, what's his name?"

"John," replied Jude.

She professionally thanked him for the information, said she would take a look at John in a minute, and then took care of Jude. Afterward, she just ignored his request about the non-existent John. Jude didn't notice. I privately suggested she might want to talk to the doctor about taking a look at Jude's medicines.

After each surgery, Jude was discharged to our home for recovery and physical therapist visits. He needed constant attention and help with his therapy. He was not an affable patient. I did my best to nurse him back to health. At the time, I continued to find walking difficult, but there was no time to talk about it with him.

During Jude's two hospital visits for hip surgeries, I became seriously sleep-deprived. I couldn't think clearly or cope well with anything. I was more stressed than I had ever been in my life.

Jude was not compliant with his physical therapist. He refused to practice his exercises and even told the therapist he didn't feel well enough to work with him on more than one occasion. Finally, at the end of my frayed rope, I called his son, Trevor, a nurse, and asked him if he could come and help me with Jude. He stayed a few days and got Jude started on the exercises and a diet regime. Thank heavens for him I thought as I went to bed for some much-needed sleep.

After these two hospitalizations however, Jude developed atrial flutter, where his heartbeat went haywire. He finally stabilized. He was put on blood thinners and other medicines and began seeing a cardiologist regularly. It happened again early in the fall. The doctors suggested ablation therapy. Jude decided not to have the procedure. He had read it was dangerous. It's true that doctors make the worst patients. They know too much and are used to giving, not taking, orders.

Unfortunately, Jude then began thinking he could die at any moment and he acted like it. Atrial flutter is in fact a serious condition if not treated, but there was treatment available.

Next, Jude developed sleep apnea and an accompanying disorder where he kicked (me) in his sleep. (At first I suspected he was kicking me on purpose! But I discovered it's a real diagnosis, restless leg syndrome.) Jude was given a mask to wear over his face. A noisy machine at our bedside had to run all night to pump oxygen under pressure into the mask while he slept. This was preferable to his loud snoring and interrupted breathing I thought.

He naturally had trouble getting used to it. He constantly ripped his mask off during the night. He would then begin snoring loudly with interrupted breathing. I would awaken and remind him to put it back on. His neurologist, who also had sleep apnea, recommended we sleep in separate rooms as he and his wife did. Jude had a fit and said he would not accept it.

It was another source of stress.

As if all these serious conditions weren't enough to take over our lives, Jude had also begun to complain about back and neck problems. He went to a specialist who told him he had disc degeneration in his neck and spine. He was warned not to lift more than fifteen pounds, mow the lawn, take the trash out, and, frankly, not do much of anything. These restrictions would go on indefinitely until Jude felt better. Interestingly, Jude was compliant with this part of the doctor's prescription! Surgery was not indicated. Exercise was.

At this point, Jude began to spend most of his time sitting in a living room chair. He watched TV, used his computer, listened to music, and read. I did all the shopping, cooking, yard work, and cleaning, necessitating a lot of walking and carrying things. More stress.

I began waiting on Jude hand and foot, out of necessity. And I didn't complain. I thought this was what I should do to help him. We were partners.

Chapter Eight: Specialists All Over Me

In the late fall of 2017, after Jude's hip surgeries and medical problems, he began to be depressed again. He discontinued his exercises. His doctors had recommended that he lose weight, and he was making no attempt to do so. He refused to stick with our modified diet. I felt he was doing nothing to help himself.

With my worsening walking and other movement issues, I was beginning to be in bad shape, physically and emotionally. I couldn't think straight. "I'm a mouse on a treadmill," I thought.

I noticed Jude was reading his medical books on a daily basis to diagnose every symptom he had, and seeing specialist after specialist. At this time, he had no further serious problems physically, but he was feeling disabled and very depressed. He told his family he could die at any moment from the heart problem. Having talked with his doctors, I felt he was dramatizing. And after all, he could choose to have the ablation done. There's an old saying, "A doctor who treats himself, has a fool for a patient."

Jude never talked about my walking problems and began criticizing me for every word out of my mouth, saying I was "bringing him down." "I'm just returning the favor," I said nastily. To add insult to injury, he began analyzing me, suggesting I needed to see a psychiatrist. You can imagine my retort. "I live with one!" But I felt he was right about getting an outside opinion. I needed help and, frankly, someone in my corner.

My walking began to get even worse, which made my mood shift from bad to horrible. I felt sadder and sadder. Jude consulted his medical books only about himself. I considered him a hypochondriac. "Hypochondrazilla!"

I had no idea what was wrong with me. My mind was spiraling out of control. I began to think I was bad and selfish. My inner thoughts centered around Jude and why he had changed from the man I had been living with. And why had I failed to make him happy? Why was I impatient with his problems? What had happened to the "in sickness" part of our promise to each other years ago? I tried my best to cheer him up but he would only smile for a little while. He made me sad. I was filled with guilt, blaming myself for his moodiness.

One day, while perusing a medical book on diagnoses, Jude noticed a section describing my walking and mood problems. He finally decided that something was wrong with me! "You have Parkinson's disease," he told me. This was because of my walking difficulties (barely shuffling along by this time and with poor balance) and my "personality change," as he put it. He suggested I see both a psychiatrist and a neurologist. And he expected me to find the doctors and make the appointments!

Thus began my descent into the world of specialists.

In December, I finally followed the first available part of Jude's advice. I called an outpatient clinical assessment center to make an appointment with a psychiatrist. After dealing with all the insurance issues, the appointment was made for January 1, 2018. Jude, who I now learned could walk pretty well, had to accompany me everywhere so I could lean on him for balance. We walked into the office and checked in. We were told to sit in the waiting room because the doctor was delayed.

Suddenly the psychiatrist came running in with a wild look on his face. He said he had to cancel the appointment because of a police matter! "I can't discuss it!" he cried. "You need to reschedule!" He then ran out. We told the flustered receptionist we would call back to reschedule and left quickly.

I said, "I don't want a hysterical psychiatrist!" (After all, I was living with one.)

"Right," said Jude.

You couldn't make this stuff up.

I found another psychiatrist, a Dr. Miller, and began seeing him. He was young and new in his work. I didn't relate to him immediately but continued to see him. "It's probably my fault," I surmised out of my constant state of insecurity. Jude sat in the waiting room while I had my appointments and made the comment at the end of each visit, "It certainly was a short visit!" This did not help my confidence any, but by then, I was experiencing extreme insecurity and stress and was too meek to make decisions. My judgment was affected. I just continued on with my appointments. I could do no more than go with the flow. Jude probably would take care of my getting the right treatment.

Meek is not an adjective anyone would have ever applied to me in the past. To the contrary, I had been known as aggressive by men, assertive by women. In the past, I was never afraid to speak my mind or stand up for myself. But now I was tired, physically weak, and confused. I relied completely on Jude. But it occurs to me now, Jude could have referred me to his own psychiatrist at the beginning.

Dr. Miller took a long-detailed history of my life. He asked me questions about my symptoms. He put me on some heavy-duty meds, to no effect except to make me feel spacey as well as depressed. I was talking so much about *me*, I was boring myself!

One day, Dr Miller leaned toward me, looked me in the eye, and said, "You're not behaving right, like my other patients. You aren't confiding in me about your feelings as much as you need to. You should probably find someone else."

I said, "Okay." I gave him no argument or questions. My meekness had no limits!

The truth is, I was old enough to be his grandmother, and that probably had a lot to do with it. However, my ego was crushed. I felt rejected.

Next, Jude stepped up and made an appointment for me with a neurologist friend of his, Dr. John Reynolds. Unbelievably, this was the same doctor who treated his sleep apnea and had recommended separate rooms for sleeping! By this time it was early in 2018.

In my history, I told Dr. Reynolds about my fall and asked

if it could have caused any of my symptoms. He said we would have to see what the tests showed, but that it was possible. He noticed my ataxia, as he called it, balance problems and dangerous gait. Dr. Reynolds watched me walk down a hall, and told me it made him afraid to watch me. It seemed at any minute I might fall!

I said, "That's *exactly* how I feel. I'm scared every time I take a step. Is there anything you can do to help me?" My eyes were tearing up at his empathetic response.

At this time Jude was still thinking I had Parkinson's Disease and said as much. Dr. Reynolds was fatherly, calm, experienced and won my confidence immediately. He said we would do a brain scan and figure out what was going on. He told me not to worry, and that I should walk only when I could do so safely, near something I could hold on to if needed. He assured me "we will get to the bottom of this." He asked Jude not to make any diagnosis until he went over the scan results with us.

Jude, however, firmly requested a copy of the scans be emailed to him as soon as available. Dr. Reynolds reluctantly agreed. Jude speaks with a great deal of authority and was still respected by other neurologists, even in retirement. In the meantime, Dr. Reynolds suggested a short term of physical therapy to see if that would help any with the severe balance problems I had developed.

He immediately scheduled appointments with a physical therapy group. Unknown to him, it turned out to be primarily a rehab group for injured athletes. Muscle bound young men were doing impossible things with weights while I, the only woman, was painstakingly riding a stationary bike and doing mild leg strengthening exercises. I gave it my all, but it was extremely discouraging to me. I desperately wanted to get better but did not.

One of the therapists noticed I was favoring my right hand and said my knuckle looked out of place. I told him about my fall and said it still hurt. He thought an X-ray of my hand would be a good idea. Finally!

The radiologist could see my swollen knuckle, but thought there was no full break indicated. He said my knuckle could have been cracked and/or jammed in my fall and, over time, had healed after migrating out of place. He showed me how to tape the first two fingers of my hand together to minimize movement and pain. That helped a lot, and I continue to do this even now whenever it hurts. I use a popsicle stick taped between my first two fingers. So something good came out of the first physical therapy debacle. It occurred to me later that an emergency room doctor could have given me this same treatment and saved me months of pain.

On March 8, Jude was in his computer room at home and suddenly began crying. I called out, "Jude, what's wrong?" He sobbed even louder and went into the bathroom, closing the door behind him. I could hear him continuing to cry. Seriously alarmed when he wouldn't answer me, I went into the living room and sat down to wait for him. My thoughts were all over the place. Had a family member died? Had his computer crashed? (He often cried over computer problems.) Had he hurt himself somehow? I knocked on the door. No answer. Only very loud crying. All I could do was wait, trying not to panic.

Finally he came out of the bathroom and blurted out, "You have Alzheimer's Disease," and began sobbing again with his hands covering his face. He didn't embrace me or try to comfort me.

He was frightening me, and I said, "What? Why are you saying that? How do you know?"

He said he had received a computer copy of my brain scan, he had looked at thousands of them, and he was sure I had it. He continued to sob even louder. I didn't show it, but I was dismayed and confused. I was getting no help from Jude. I wanted him to reassure me, tell me he loved me and it would be all right, that we would be together in this. But he wanted me to comfort him! "If it moves, you comfort it." But not this time.

Suddenly, irrationally, I became very calm. I reminded him, "We have an appointment with Dr. Reynolds tomorrow. We should discuss the diagnosis with him." Jude reluctantly agreed, though he still was upset. He made himself a drink and then had a few more before bed. He had begun drinking to excess again. I knew I would have to handle the news alone that night and maybe for the near future. It was a lonely feeling.

I sat in my living room in the darkness after Jude went up to bed alone. I was "on hold," not really realizing what it meant. I didn't believe I had Alzheimer's Disease. I couldn't wrap my head around what he said or consider the consequences. It briefly crossed my mind: did it mean I would end up in a vegetative state? It didn't bear thinking about. Of course, I did think about it as I tried to go to sleep that night.

I lay awake saying to myself "I have Alzheimer's" over and over, but it still didn't sink in. My mind circled the topic but couldn't seem to understand that this referred to me and was not some abstract diagnosis to research and analyze. I just didn't know what to do. I decided there was nothing to do now. Or, maybe ever. "Just accept what happens and do the best I can." I was actually calmer than I should have been in hindsight. I don't know why. I really didn't grasp the diagnosis. I felt strange and unclear about what would happen next.

Whenever something bad has happened to me or my family, I've not gone to pieces immediately. First I would think what to do, and afterwards I would be afraid or upset.

My brother David had several heart attacks, and each time I acted calm, his "MUCH older, wiser sister (as he jokingly calls me)." I made upbeat hospital visits to cheer him up, though I was deeply worried. I know from previous job experiences that I have always seen problems as challenges and love solving them. I am known by my family as the one who never panics.

This was different, though. I didn't know if I would have any control over the outcome. I worried, I ruminated, then panicked, then reassured myself, then denied, then found some measure of acceptance—that was my endless first night. I finally fell asleep for a few hours.

The next day the first thought I had upon awakening, was

"I have Alzheimer's Disease." Immediately the thought struck me, "I might have something seriously wrong with me." I wasn't used to this. I had been reasonably active and healthy in the past.

We met with Dr. Reynolds. I went into the room alone with him and told him that Jude looked at the scans, told me I had Alzheimer's Disease, and couldn't stop crying. Dr. Reynolds took Jude into another room before we all three met. He calmed Jude down before the meeting.

When we sat down to discuss the scans, Dr. Reynolds said he could see damage in my brain, but to him it looked like adult-onset hydrocephalus, two pockets of water in the middle of my brain, which could have caused all my symptoms, mental and physical. It could have developed as a reaction to my head injury. I could have had a concussion. He said researchers are now publishing research about concussions later manifesting as behaviors which are mistakenly diagnosed as Alzheimer's Disease.

Jude disagreed, saying he saw the classic signs of Alzheimer's Disease. They debated the merits of each diagnosis. I asked Jude about the fall, but he, stuck on his own diagnosis, overruled Dr. Reynolds and said he didn't think my fall had led to hydrocephalus. He wouldn't even consider any other diagnosis. I was in the dark, depending on Dr. Reynolds and Jude. Of course, I preferred Dr. Reynolds' diagnosis, but I couldn't imagine myself overruling Jude. We had trusted each other enough to sign over medical powers of attorney and advanced directives in the past.

Dr. Reynolds asked me to start physical therapy with another group which specialized in patients with balance issues and walking difficulties. He also suggested I try yoga for balance. He set up the physical therapy referral and made an appointment with himself for May 29, two months hence. He wanted to give me the full benefit of the physical therapy, before we would assess my progress and diagnosis.

He was hoping that my walking and balance problems would improve.

He said, **"You don't act like an Alzheimer's patient. Your cognitive abilities seem normal to me."**
I felt better immediately. Jude said nothing. Why didn't I see how little he was involved with me? Because I wasn't thinking clearly.

The new PT group had a very small room but many rotating physical therapists. I saw six physical therapists over nine physical therapy sessions, during which I became very discouraged. I seemed unable to make any improvement. I wobbled walking around bowling pins, laps around the room, standing and balancing on one leg with my eyes closed, and most other prescribed activities. I continuously felt I was going to fall without a therapist standing with me and almost did several times. I wasn't getting much individual attention. Each time I visited I had a different therapist, with a slightly different approach. The therapists were very interested in socializing with each other, seemingly more than helping the patients. However, I did enjoy listening them tell each other stories of their weekend activities, mostly involving the opposite sex. I enjoy watching other people.

Finally, the instructors had a conference with Jude. I wasn't invited to this conference, and Jude didn't share the results with me. I was afraid to ask. I believed my prognosis was so bad no one wanted to tell me. Probably they confirmed I had Parkinson's or Alzheimer's Disease. I knew what they were and what it would mean.

I was given a bright pink T-shirt emblazoned with the name of their practice in recognition of the completion of my therapy. At least it was something to take home, if not improvement, I thought cynically. But I knew I had tried my best.

I signed up for a gentle yoga class at the local YMCA, and, since I was able to hold on to a chair for balance, I loved it. We learned relaxation techniques which caused the sessions to end in a blissful, relaxed state. I began trying the yoga techniques, particularly deep breathing, at home on my own. It helped calm me down when I began to worry about my future. I wasn't sure I had Alzheimer's. My cognitive skills seemed the same as always to me, though I had little insight into my behavior. But my walking hadn't improved.

When we met with Dr. Reynolds on May 29, he told us he was retiring in a few weeks. This was distressing information. His replacement was a young woman who had just completed her residency with him. She seemed pleasant and eager to continue trying to figure out what was wrong with me.

But before we left, Dr. Reynolds reassured Jude and me about my future. He recommended another neurologist well-known for diagnosing and treating ataxia and other movement problems such as Alzheimer's Disease and hydrocephalus. He suggested we make an appointment for an evaluation with Dr Ishtar Medzul, who, like Dr. Reynolds, was on the staff of the medical school associated with University Regional Hospital. He was well-known in the field and was an Associate Professor of the Department of Neurology. Dr. Reynolds made a final appointment with himself for June 25 to check with us for closure.

After this meeting with Dr. Reynolds, Jude did not make the referral to Dr. Medzul, but referred me to a new psychiatric group, friends of his. He convinced me that this group would help me feel better, though I said, "I think walking better would help me the most." Jude didn't find my comment funny. He hardly ever talked to me about my condition or asked me how I was doing. I was too discombulated to notice it.

CHAPTER NINE: My Son Comes Home

One night about this time, out of the blue, my son Andrew called. It was a year after he and his fiancée Larisa had moved to Bend, Oregon to live. Andrew had two jobs, working as a chef in a five-star restaurant and part time in a second restaurant. He had told me how much he had learned and how much he loved his work in Oregon. He sent pictures of beautiful dishes he had created. Recently he had been contacted by a television cooking show interested in his work from seeing his on-line postings. He and Larisa loved Oregon: hiking, going to the beach, mountain climbing and running with their dog. It was a joyous time for them.

Andrew suddenly asked, "Are you okay, Mom? You haven't sounded like yourself recently."

I replied honestly, "Not so well." This was a first. I always acted upbeat with Andrew, not wanting to worry him about anything.

I told him about my walking problems and the depressed state they had caused, but not about the possible Alzheimer's diagnosis.

"Are you and Jude getting along?"

I said, "Not really. This is a stressful time."

He asked quietly, "Do you need me to come home, Mom?"

My voice trembled. I told him "No." I said, "I just can't ask you to do that." He was starting out in a career that he had worked hard for years to achieve. He had moved across the country for the opportunity. It was the beginning of what looked like a successful career in a field he loved.

Andrew said not to worry about it. He said he could get a job in any number of good restaurants here at home. He was concerned because I was not a complainer. He wanted me to make a decision right then. I said I would need to think about it overnight.

I have loved Andrew with all my heart since the joyous

morning he was born. We were very close through all his years. After my divorce from his father, I was the parent who took care of him during the school year.

And now this amazing, loving offer from my son. I couldn't believe he would be willing to make such a sacrifice. My readers will find it hard to believe that he would offer to leave his job and come home. There is no doubt that God had a hand in this, as well as Andrew's sweet and giving soul.

I immediately felt safer and better about my future. It's hard to explain. Inside, I was less up tight. I felt there was someone on my side who had my interest at heart. In fact, I realized I had lost my previous blind trust in Jude and often felt he didn't care for me. When I discussed the offer with Jude, he said, "Ask Andrew to come." I should have realized that this was the handwriting on the wall. What I thought at the time, though, was that I must be deathly ill if Jude wanted Andrew to move back home.

After considering it overnight, I called Andrew and told him I needed him and asked him if he really could come home. I told him about the likely Alzheimer's diagnosis. I said I would not ask this lightly and believed he could help me get better.

He said, "Absolutely yes." I asked if Larisa was okay with this, and he said she was totally supportive.

Never in my life have I felt so relieved!

I will never forget how gracious and loving Andrew was about this. He told me this was what he wanted to do, and it was the right thing for me and for him. He wanted to take care of me as I had taken care of him for most of his life. What a sweet thing to say. I felt wonderful, deep down in my heart. I knew he would begin making arrangements to move back home and this would be good for me.

About the same time, things had moved on rapidly with Jude's friend, a new psychiatrist, Dr. Jackson Kennedy, and his counselor cohorts. I would go to my appointments and do nothing but cry. I would come out of the office into the waiting room with swollen red eyes. I had frankly expressed my feelings about my worsening relationship with Jude and my possible diagnosis. I had felt I must be open with Dr. Kennedy for the sake of my own fragile mental health. Jude, waiting for me, would then be called in to see his friend without me.

Jude was spending a lot of time alone with the psychiatrist, and my medicines were changed frequently. I wasn't feeling better, maybe even worse. I was beginning to feel more spacey and disoriented.

"What if Jude's advice is making me worse?" I wondered. Thinking back, I believe it did so. And I was feeling infantilized by the private meetings of two lofty doctors from which I was excluded. My anger began to build, focused on Jude. I just didn't have the energy or wherewithal to fight what was happening.

I anxiously waited for Andrew to arrive.

He did so in June and moved into an apartment down the street. A friend of his offered it to him and Larisa as a temporary measure.

The first thing Andrew did was take me to my long-time primary physician, Dr. Hanes, because I suspected I had a urinary tract infection. But my urine was clear. A complete physical check-up showed me to be in good health except for walking problems. He was Jude's doctor also, and we didn't discuss the problems in our relationship or my mental state. We three talked about what to do. Dr. Hanes prescribed a walker for assistance and suggested getting a wheelchair. He ordered a handicapped sticker for my car. Being an endocrinologist as well as a family practitioner, he did a complete blood panel. All my results were within normal ranges.

After we talked a while, he told Andrew and me he couldn't see any signs of Alzheimer's Disease, but in any case at my age it would develop slowly. He said I was healthy and would probably live a long time. He said he had known a lot of people with that diagnosis who had lived rich and normal lives. This was his opinion formed from treating thousands of patients over his career. Andrew and I immediately felt more hopeful.

The second thing Andrew and I did was to visit a lawyer, making Andrew my Power of Attorney, and Medical Power of Attorney. I signed papers saying what decisions I wanted made in medical emergencies. We also drew up a will. We explained my possible diagnosis. The lawyer asked me some questions and said he thought I was *compos mentis* and the documents would be legally binding. He told us I didn't show any signs of Alzheimer's to him, and he had worked with such patients and their families previously.

The third thing Andrew did was to ask me, "Is there anything we can do to reduce your stress level?" I asked, "Could we go to Wrightsville Beach for a few days?" This was a favorite beach of ours in North Carolina and only a three-hour drive. Jude had told us that he was going to the shore for a week with his son Phillip. (I had not been invited.) So this would be a good time for a weekend trip, we decided. After we made our reservations, Jude said he would go with us. I said, "No." I firmly explained we had made plans for the two of us since we thought he would be out of town. I was proud of myself for standing firm on this, because Jude unrelentingly tried to make me feel guilty, saying his beach trip with his son had fallen through. But I knew the time alone with my son would reduce my stress.

Andrew and I rented a wheelchair and had a marvelous time. We went sightseeing and even out onto the beach. I have some goofy pictures of us at an aquarium in front of a mural of a huge shark attacking us. We both look happy. People we passed smiled at us. I felt a lot better. Totally relaxed and relieved to be spending time with my son. Larisa visited her parents for the first time since she had returned from Oregon. Everyone was happy with the plans, except Jude. I didn't care! I desperately needed relief.

A strange thing had happened at the beach. Andrew had left me in the wheelchair near the bathhouse, while he briefly returned to his room. I decided I would use the bathroom. I tried to walk up the ramp, holding on the wooden rail. I couldn't grip the rail, so I knelt down and began crawling upward. This seemed a reasonable thing to do. A minister and his family were walking by. The minister began praying aloud for me! He said kindly, "Don't worry, you'll get better." His words made me feel better, so I said, "Amen!" He asked if he could help me. Andrew walked up at that moment, thanked him and helped me up to the ladies' room. He didn't seem annoyed that I had tried to crawl up the ramp by myself.

Soon after the beach trip, Andrew went with me to a meeting of the psychiatrists, counselors, Andrew, Jude and me. Alzheimer's was not discussed. They were not neurologists and this was not in their area of expertise. Specialists are trained in a limited field of study. Dr. Kennedy decided to add Abilify to my cocktail of medicines. It is an anti-psychotic drug used to treat schizophrenia, among other things. Some psychiatrists treat depression with it "off label." Yes, I was depressed but I had real reasons for being so. I wasn't feeling well physically or mentally but didn't know enough to question why I should take this drug, which Jude took in large doses.

They told me I might be bipolar. *Was no stone going to be left unturned?* Had Jude suggested this? Andrew asked some good questions, but this was his first experience with the team of my doctors, and he asked Jude what he thought. I personally had seen Jude on his high dose of Abilify become totally unresponsive. Far be it for anyone on the team to ask my opinion. I was too intimidated and weak-willed to speak up.

Jude felt we should try the Abilify, so my son reluctantly went along with the recommendation. I could tell Andrew was uncomfortable not knowing anything about the medicine or its pharmacology. My possible diagnosis was a surprise to him. He did not think that I was bipolar. Nor did I. Andrew had majored in chemistry and biochemistry in college, and he knew that chemicals can affect older people in idiosyncratic ways. And I was taking a lot of chemicals. He told me privately that he would research the medicines I was taking. The doctor's office called the prescription in to the pharmacy.

After taking the Abilify for one day, I was in the kitchen

33

when I saw a tiny, smiling, blue wizard running around. He was darling, and I loved him. Andrew and Larisa walked in from grocery shopping for us, and I, delighted, showed them the blue wizard, giggling continuously at his antics. The spritely wizard immediately jumped into the grocery bags and was running around the celery!

Andrew calmly said, "Mom, I don't see him."

"He's right there on the celery!" I said.

But Andrew said calmly, "No one's there."

"Yes he is!" I pointed my finger at him. "Are you saying I'm seeing things?" I was very upset, because I really loved my blue wizard and was still watching him, this time as he ran up the refrigerator, perched on the top and grinned at us. I didn't want to lose him.

Andrew went in to talk to Jude who was in the next room saying nothing, and who did not come into the kitchen to investigate. Andrew came back into the kitchen looking perturbed and said we should call my psychiatrist since Jude didn't seem concerned and didn't think the Abilify reaction was a problem. Andrew did. So did Larisa. Because of their reaction, I realized something was wrong with me.

I called Dr. Kennedy's office and explained what was happening. The *receptionist,* without consulting anyone, told me to take an increased dose of Abilify! I was outraged and repeated out loud what she had said. Andrew and Larisa looked incredulous, and Jude called out from the other room, "That's what I would do." I told the receptionist that was not acceptable, and I was not about to do it. I was apparently seeing things that were not there and was not going to add any other symptoms to my evening! I hung up. Other than the wizard, I could still be rational.

I called out to Jude, "You're crazy! I'm not taking another Abilify pill!"

Andrew and Larisa agreed totally with me. I had known Jude was a narcissist (he confided this to me one time but flippantly added "everybody has to be something"). I could now see that he was totally into himself. This was all about him, and he no longer wanted to bother with me. It appeared he didn't love me. However, I didn't make it an issue because my son was there to take care of me now. My previous feelings for Jude were far from my consciousness now. I was in survival mode.

I stopped the Abilify, heard beautiful music outside of my window while in bed that night, but both it and my friend the blue wizard were gone the next afternoon. I forgot to be disappointed. It was the right thing to do. I was on a lot of meds. Andrew was shocked at the number and type of drugs prescribed for me. He made an appointment for me to see a new private psychiatrist as soon as possible.

Some of this next period of time is indistinct in my memory.

As I said, I was on a lot of psychiatric medicines, and I was getting worse. I can vaguely remember things that happened at that time. I was going in and out of a fog. I was starting to be out of my head part of the time. I didn't even think to define what was happening to me.

One night I was in the bathtub and couldn't get out. I was confused. I tried and tried to figure it out but couldn't. I called for Jude to help me. He came in and grabbed me by my upper arms and yanked on them to try to pull me up. I screamed, "You're killing me! Please stop!"

"Quiet down!" Jude said sternly. He said he was afraid the neighbors would call the police. He phoned Andrew and asked him to come right away and help get me out. Andrew immediately ran over. He knew how to get my arms around his neck and stand up, bringing me up with him. I hate that this image of me naked is probably imprinted forever in his brain. As I reflect now, I wonder why Jude didn't put a towel around me before Andrew arrived.

I learned that doctors are not trained in details of patient care.

Jude didn't have any knowledge of how to help me move around. Andrew had studied exercise physiology and knew what to do. Jude watched him and could have learned the techniques if he wanted to. But he was happy to have Andrew take care of my needs. Less pressure on him to provide care. This bathtub incident happened once again, and Jude called EMTs this time. I remember being naked and wet, with Jude and three men in full uniform crowded into the bathroom. They stood around looking at me discussing what to do. Finally, one did exactly what Andrew had done. Though he was kind and patient, it took him a while to persuade me to follow his directions because I was afraid. I remember the feel of the hard clasps on his uniform against my naked body. I didn't know enough at the time to be embarrassed. I am now, though. I have no memory of what happened next. Did they dry me off, did they put me in my nightgown, did they get me into bed? I've blacked out the memory.

When I think back on this, I'm angry at Jude. He was not thoughtful and caring when I needed him. I never once during that time felt loving attention from him. Thank God for Andrew!

I was too out of it to know how seriously I was deteriorating. Days seemed a blur to me, and I don't have memory of details except as I'm relating. Some events stand out in my mind as clearly as the bathtub problem.

I started to have trouble getting up into my bed. It was high off the ground. Jude put a small, light-weight plastic stepstool beside the bed and told me to stand on it, bend over and push myself into the bed. I tried and the stool tipped over backward, almost causing me to fall. I was terrified and wouldn't try it again. Jude couldn't think of anything else except yank on my arms which I would not let him do. I also wouldn't let him call Andrew or EMTs. Enough!

It was up to me. After thinking about it for a while, I took a short running start and dived up into the bed! This was one of my favorite things to do as a child, and my muscle memory made it work. Jude was horrified, but I was laughing. And, in the bed. A small victory, but important to me. I still remember the pitiful feeling of accomplishment I had at that moment. I was proud of myself. Not a frequent feeling in those days. I continued to get into bed this way until I was inexplicably hospitalized.

CHAPTER TEN: The House of Pain and Fog

Jude had me hospitalized on June 30 by Dr. Kennedy. I barely remember it. I was admitted to County Memorial Hospital for testing due to my movement difficulties and personality changes. This took place when Andrew and Larisa were out of town visiting her parents. When notified by the hospital (not Jude), Andrew was surprised and alarmed but authorized the admission. He was deeply worried about me and thought a complete battery of tests would be useful. Also, my meds would be checked and a list made for him. He made plans to return immediately.

I have only hazy memories of what happened over the next five days. Again there were clear moments from time to time. I remember being taken on a stretcher into a large unoccupied room where I was left. Suddenly someone's arm reached into the room and turned the light off, and I was in total darkness. I had no idea what to do or where I was, and I was really frightened. After what seemed a long while, I heard voices and began to yell, "Help!" At last a man in white with a stethoscope around his neck stuck his head in the door, turned on the light, and said with a surprised gasp, "I didn't know anyone was in here!"

I remember looking at a man in white against white curtains who asked me my name. I didn't know and said so.

Jude apparently had told the doctors of my problems walking, getting into and out of bed and the bathroom, and his take on my brain scan, Alzheimer's Disease. I was given a battery of tests over those five days, of which I have no memory at all. I only know what they were because recently I looked back over my insurance claims. An EKG, an ECG, an MRI, a CAT scan, a PET scan and a chest x-ray were all performed. It seems no scan was omitted!

I don't remember anyone visiting me at the hospital. I do, however, have some haunting memories of this time. I could hear terrible sounds at night.

Once I heard a man yelling loud and creative curses at the top of his lungs. He was demanding someone come and help him. His voice echoed up and down the halls. I felt afraid and going to sleep was impossible. After what seemed a disturbingly long time, a nurse must have gone to his room, because I could hear him haranguing her for a cigarette. She firmly told him he could not have one. She said if he didn't calm down she was going to take him to the mental ward. He continued and indeed, must have been moved. Things quieted down, and I fell asleep. The next day I heard two nurses talking in my room, saying that he was demented and wouldn't be back on that hall.

It seems that I didn't really need to ask nurses about anything happening in the halls around me, because I could hear them talking about it in front of me the same or next day.

Somehow, I knew they shouldn't be talking about him in front of me, but it was helpful to me. It reinforced that what I heard really happened.

Another night I thought I heard voices of older boys running toward me. I thought I was in a building beside my church, and they were going to hurt me. I apparently was making noises. The door to my room opened, the light was turned on, and two nurses came in to reassure me. They reminded me where I was and said that I was just having a nightmare. I was safe, they assured me. They left a light on for me. What a terrible dream it was! In it I was terrified. Perhaps these were my true but repressed feelings at the time of what Alzheimer's could do to me.

When I was discharged from the hospital, Andrew and Jude were given my diagnosis as Alzheimer's Disease. Hydrocephalus was not mentioned, nor was my fall, Andrew says now. No one talked to me about my condition, believing I would not be cognizant enough to discuss it.

Apparently, Andrew had begun researching and looking for

available resources locally. He had ordered a permanent wheelchair, a bedside potty, and a hospital bed to be delivered to the house. He had a Home Care Assessment team scheduled to assess the possibility of someone caring for me at home. Jude made an Emergency Plan in case I had to go to a Nursing Home. My sister and three brothers were notified and began to do research from out of town. I had no idea what was going on. Andrew kindly did not think it advisable to talk to me about my diagnosis at that time. Apparently, I had forgotten about Alzheimer's for the time being.

Four days went by after the hospitalization. I wasn't aware of the days passing or what I was doing. I was in dream world.

But I have a vivid recollection at the end of that time of being at home in my bedroom, lying on my bed in excruciating pain. It was night, my room was dark, and I was groaning. I kept calling out, "Jude, Jude!" I could hear Jude and his son Trevor, a registered nurse, in the next room laughing and joking.

Finally, after what seemed like hours, Trevor came into my room. He might have come in periodically to place me on the potty chair beside my bed. I was in the hospital bed Andrew ordered by then, and I couldn't get the side rail down. I had to slide down to the end of the bed and get out the short opening at the foot. When I think of Trevor sitting there watching me struggle without assistance, I can see now how much he and Jude were indifferent to me. At least Trevor should have lowered my side rails and helped me out of bed. Jude had promised me one time that if I were sick he would take care of me, even to wiping my bottom. He said he was used to anything because he had been a doctor. But that night he forgot to love and care for me. That night Trevor became very familiar with my intimate female parts.

I could not urinate or pass anything. I was in bad pain when I tried to no avail. The entire night went by with no success. I was in agony.

I'm told Jude called Andrew the next morning, who came over and said angrily, "I'm taking Mother to the Emergency

Room immediately. I'm calling Dr. Medzul to contact a specialist to meet us there."

What was wrong with Jude and Trevor? Were they not trained medical professionals? What were they thinking? Why was I allowed to lie in agony overnight? Did they hope I would die? I'm terribly hurt by their neglect of basic human kindness and their lack of action.

I'm furious when I think of what could have happened to me. In fact, a lot did happen. I was seriously ill.

I was quickly given an ultrasound by a urologist, Andrew later told me. I needed emergency treatment. I was immediately admitted to the hospital. I remember none of this.

The next thing I do remember is lying on a bed. I could see curtains shielding me and could hear voices talking in low tones behind them. It seemed like a lot of men, maybe doctors, maybe Andrew and Jude, I presume now. Then some women in white came into my room and said, "You have to be catheterized right now!"

It didn't immediately hit me what that meant. They yanked up my gown, spread my legs, held them down and picked up an aluminum, one-inch strip with jaws in the middle. They discussed how it was a new model designed to open the urethra fully. They pulled my genitals apart and laid the jagged strip on my urethra to pry it open. Then they inserted a tube. I was extremely sore from my infection. I remember crying out loudly, "Oh, please stop, please stop. It hurts!" They said they were sorry. I felt I was being tortured with no hope of rescue. Again I was in agony. I felt totally alone. I can hardly bear to think about it even now.

My doctors and son have told me that I had a critical bladder infection that almost killed me. My bladder was the size of a basketball! It was filled with thick gray pus, which had to be removed as soon as possible. Someone showed me what it looked like. No wonder I was in pain! I had to be catheterized every three hours, and each time a large bag at the end of my bed had to be full before they stopped. It took a long time to fill up. Then I lay in my bed dreading the next procedure. The time went by in a haze of pain. I couldn't sleep. I grew to dread the sliver of light entering the room as the door opened, because it meant the grim nurses were back. I learned that some nurses were better than others and begged for them. There was one older, kind nurse who was very gentle and didn't hurt me as much. I begged her to do all the procedures. Of course, she wasn't on duty 24 hours a day. I asked her to show the other nurses how to do the procedures. I am told I had eight catheterizations, one every three hours. Each one was more painful than the last.

Strange, cloudy memories cross my mind of this second time in the hospital. Nothing is chronological, and it seems like a movie with missing parts. Strangely, I wasn't afraid at all after the catheterizations were over, because I had forgotten that something else terrible was happening to me. I was thinking only how grateful I was to be relieved of the awful pain I had been experiencing.

There was a great, silent space around me. I knew that I was a person inside this body I was lying in, that people in white coats were coming in frequently and asking questions, that they were young men, and that time was passing. I had a high fever. I remember Andrew coming in once and reassuring me that everything would be all right, saying, "Don't worry Mom. I'm here. The doctors will take good care of you. They've told me you're already getting better."

Jude later told me he was there, too, but I don't remember seeing him.

From my bed I could see through a window that looked across to another wing of the hospital, perpendicular to mine, with a long balcony. At night, a man would come out and sit in a chair. I stared at him each night for what seemed like endless hours. I thought he was an astronomer looking through a telescope at the stars. Then one night I saw a red light, and thought he was looking at me through a camera taking pictures. I was anxious and worried about it. I wondered if he was going to come to my room to hurt me. Again, I didn't tell this to anyone, but I still vividly remember it. Maybe I was hallucinating because of my high fever.

Doctors and nurses came and went every day. They would openly discuss me as if I weren't there. They looked at each other and not at me.

Between doctor visits, I would stare out my window at the clouds going past. It occupied my time. Sometimes it rained, other times it was sunny. Sometimes the clouds were scudding in the sky, blown by the wind. I enjoyed watching the weather every day, and it fully occupied my mind. I was never bored. It's hard for me now to believe how satisfied I was by just idly lying in bed looking out the window, daydreaming. It was restful.

Groups of doctors would troop into my room several times a day, disturbing my peaceful reflections, asking me questions which seemed to come out of left field. I discovered later they were Dr. Medzul's neurology residents. They were always asking the same questions, he told me. They asked me my full name. Sometimes I could answer them. They had put a white board on the wall of my room showing my name, the date, where I was, and my room number. But I hadn't noticed or paid attention to it.

Finally one of the doctors said, "You know, you can look up on the wall at the white board for the answers if you want to." I said, noticing the board for the first time, "That would be cheating, wouldn't it?"

He said that was why they put the board there in my line of sight. After a while, I peeked at the board as he suggested, and the doctors were pleased at my answers, saying, "Very good." I was ridiculously pleased at my accomplishment.

It seemed I was in suspended time. I do remember nurses trying to get me to walk into the bathroom beside my bed. They grabbed my upper arms to hold me and pull me out of bed. It hurt my arms. They apparently hadn't been trained how to lift a patient. This attempt at walking was complicated by the fact that I had to wear hospital socks. I wear a size 5 ½ shoe and the socks were about three inches too long. They were loose, flopped around my feet and were slippery on the floor. The nurses looked for a smaller size but said there was nothing smaller. I tried to explain how to lift me up from the bed and to let me wear my tennis shoes. But I was ignored.

Black and blue bruises appeared on my upper arms from nurses holding tightly onto them and on my lower arms from IV's. These were scary and terrible looking and ultimately took over a year to go away.

One day without notice I was suddenly wheeled down the hall to a room full of doctors seated down each side of a long table. Sitting up was disorienting because I had been bedbound for so long. I was clothed immodestly in my hospital gown. I remember this experience clearly. Dr. Medzul was there and was moderating the group. He sat beside me and said he would be asking me a lot of questions.

He said this was different testing from before, and I should do the best I could. He said some of the test was hard, and I was not expected to know all the answers. He was looking at me kindly right in the eye, at least. He said the men in the room were all doctors who were on his team and were there to help find out what was going on with me.

Then the testing began.

Of the tests I remember, the following were the highlights: I was asked my name and by now, I knew it. The usual time, date, and year questions were asked. Bingo! Then things got a little harder. I was asked to walk forward, backward and stand with my eyes closed. I wouldn't even try standing with my eyes closed. I had to point to various parts of my body, tell if I felt pin pricks, follow objects with my eyes, touch my fingers together in front of my nose, and many more physical things.

I was given 3 words to remember later, then given an oral list of words to repeat immediately after it was read slowly to me. I was asked to draw a clock, copy a three-dimensional geometrical figure, draw a square, a house and other objects. I was shown pictures and asked to name the objects. Then I was asked the three words. Oops!

I had become extremely anxious. Dr. Medzul said to count

backward from 100 by 7's. I got to 93. He gave me a piece of paper with numbers from 1 to 20 scattered randomly over the paper. I was to connect the numbers in ascending order without lifting the pencil from the paper, as fast as I could. This was followed immediately by a sheet of paper with numbers interspersed with letters. I was to connect them in alternating ascending order without lifting the pencil. It was timed. I did well on these two tests.

Then came the final question. "Name as many words starting with 'F' that you can in one minute." I immediately went blank. Suddenly a word occurred to me. "Fuck," I sang out loudly. I heard a snort from down the table. Lord, of all the words in the English language, did I really say that? I began to think it was funny and started giggling. Probably that was not appropriate. In my defense, I did think of a few more words. I was proud of *forensic and follicle.*

After the neurological testing, Andrew was told again I had Alzheimer's Disease.

I have no memory of leaving afterward or returning to my hospital room. It's disconcerting to me, as I think back over those days, that there are so many totally blank spaces. Why remember one thing so clearly and not the next? And then days go by with no memory at all of what happened during that time, or even that time went by. That's Alzheimer's Disease, the doctor later said to my son and me.

Dr. Medzul said I would need to go to a nursing and rehabilitation facility after this hospitalization. Andrew was given a list of such homes nearby and began calling. All were full, until he came to the end of the list. He visited and said, against all odds, it was clean and quite nice. He made arrangements for me to move there.

CHAPTER ELEVEN: I Move Into a Home For Zombies

I was in the hospital after my testing until on July 20, I am told, Dr. Medzul and Andrew came into my hospital room to see me. Dr. Medzul said he was releasing me with some medicine which would completely clear up my bladder infection. He told Andrew I would need to wear Depends. He was discharging me to a skilled nursing and rehabilitation facility so I could rest and receive proper nursing care, physical and occupational therapy, and support counseling. He made it sound like a pleasant vacation. It was okay with me.

Andrew said it was a good idea, and in the meantime he would get my home ready for when I returned. He said this was not a permanent move, because "I will never leave you in a nursing home, Mom." Dr. Medzul and Andrew both said when I was better we would talk about my diagnosis. An ambulance was called to transport me to the nursing home.

I clearly remember the ambulance ride to the facility with two young drivers. Andrew was not in the ambulance with me as he had to pick up my wheelchair from home. Ambulances and I are no longer friends. I was not strapped in tightly and was afraid I was going to fall off of the stretcher when I was slung from side to side. There was road construction, and there was swerving and jouncing. The driver and attendant were up front talking and joking. I thought they were driving too fast around curves. I felt like any minute I would fall onto the floor sideways. I told them about it, and they briefly turned their heads and one of them said, "You won't fall out."

The ride lasted forever, and I was a nervous wreck when I arrived at the Nursing Home, where Andrew was waiting at the door with my wheelchair. "Thank God," I thought, "at last."

My fear of falling was reinforced during this drive. It persists to an extent today.

45

Andrew told me later he checked me in. It's funny when I realize that I began to remember things during times Andrew was around. He was my only trusted person and I relaxed when he was with me. His coming home to help was indeed a miracle for me, a blessing from God.

The admitting nurses asked if I could walk at all, and Andrew said, "Somewhat." They asked me to do so, and I almost fell. They said disapprovingly to Andrew, taking notes on a clipboard, "She can't walk at all. She's definitely a fall risk." Then Andrew wheeled me to my room. He apparently knew exactly where it was.

He had packed some clothes for me, brought Depends with him, and got me moved in. We talked for a bit about the room, which I did notice was huge, a room for two, in which I would live alone. "No one to have to worry about," Andrew said. The room was as large as my bedroom at home!

There were chairs and a lounge chair, a wall TV, a wardrobe, a bureau, a side table, a hospital bed and a potty chair beside my bed. There was my own wheelchair. There was also a huge bathroom with a wide door and a wheelchair-accessible shower. A large window with curtains was at the far end of the room. During this quick tour, nothing much registered with me at the time, but later I saw how privileged I was to have such a spacious room.

Then Andrew left to go home. He said he loved me and would see me the next day. He left me his phone number and my cell phone on the side table by the bed. I had no idea of the concept of cell phone. I clung to him and told him I wish he didn't have to go, and I couldn't wait to see him the next day. I felt bereft when he left.

It was nighttime. The next person to come in out of the wilderness beyond time outside of my room was a lady in white who gave me my meds. She told me her name and seemed sweet but authoritative. She said sternly, "Do *not* get out of bed without calling for help. " This was confusing to me. Why would I want to get out of my bed?

She told me this was so I would not fall. This was a strict

rule. "No falling," she said. "This is very important for your safety. You don't want to fall and break a leg, do you?"

"Hardly," I thought, clinging to the sides of the bed by then. I asked meekly "What if I have to use the bathroom?" It had suddenly occurred to me I might have to go to the bathroom during the night.

In response she pointed out the potty chair beside my bed to the left and showed me how to get into it. I was to turn left in my bed and get my legs hanging over the side. Then I should reach across the chair with both arms, one on each chair arm. I should lean on the chair arms and stand up. Then I had to turn around switching arms so I could lean back and sit down. There was toilet paper to the side. To get back in bed, I was to stand up, switch arms while turning around, lean on the chair arms, then move sideways to the bed and turn around. Then I was to back up and sit on the bed, bringing my legs up after me.

If you're confused, so was I! There was no way I understood and little hope that I would remember her instructions. I promptly forgot. And good, because she then said, "But, push the call button beside you before you get out of bed to use the potty." She had to show me again where the call button was (woven into the rail on the right of my bed) and she put my hand on it. That was pretty clear I thought.

She told me that in the middle of the night a nurse would wake me to give me more meds. Then in the morning someone would bring me breakfast to eat in bed. I would be shown what to do all day, and I should not worry about my schedule.

The only thing I was worried about was how to use the potty chair if no one answered the buzzer! She left my room, turning off the overhead lights but leaving a soft light on in the ceiling of the hall to the bathroom in my room. It was the perfect night light for reassurance in the night, which I would soon need. But at the time, I felt safe. Unfortunately, that was not to last through the night.

Alas, I discovered this reassuring nursing home protocol did not continue for long. As the days went by, I noticed seriously long responses to my call button, and I would have to wait so long I often urinated or worse in my "diaper" as they called it. They would scold me loudly as if I were a naughty child when this happened. They would lay me face-down across the bed, pull down my diaper, wipe me with a warm cloth, and put a new diaper on me. The expression on their faces as they turned me over and straightened or changed my sheets I will not forget. I do remember my acute embarrassment. Imagine if I had a roommate! I tried to reassure myself that they did this all the time. There is just no way to think about this without a red face. I now think I should have moved heaven and earth to draw a smiley face on my derriere for them.

Remember the soothing night light? That very first night, I was startled out of a sound sleep by the horrible sound of men howling in the night somewhere outside my room! Disoriented and terrified I heard the noise coming from my left and close by. The howling alternated with spooky high-pitched wailing sounds. There were male high-pitched maniacal calls of "Oh God, please help me," and "I'm trapped," "Let me out," "I'm hurt. Aiee. I want to get out of here. Ouwoo!" These phrases rang out amid wordless screams and howling. I thought the crowd of men was getting closer to me by the minute. I began panicking. It was a cacophony of many screams at the same time, and it frightened me beyond words.

"Monsters, and getting closer and closer," I knew. I was frantic.

Afraid to move or even to push a button to summon help, I made myself stay as quiet and still as possible. I was hardly breathing. I tried to stop my trembling. I went into survival mode. I knew any noise from my room would attract the attention of this crowd of screaming banshees, and they would surely come and get me. I lay frozen, listening intently, waiting, waiting.

A nurse finally came in with my late night medications. Turning on the light, she said, "Time for your night meds. Oh, you're awake. Can't you sleep?" I told her I had heard men yelling, thinking I might have dreamed it. She said blithely, "Oh, that's the men in the mental hospital up yonder. Don't

She showed me how to use the TV. I actually got used to Yvonne's nightly calls after a while, just as I did with the mentally ill men up the hill.

Once Andrew was visiting in the early evening. and she began her shrieking. Andrew glanced at me inquisitively. I quietly explained. As she went on and on, his lips twitched and then mine did, as the sound was so uncanny. We begin laughing silently. Gallows humor. Again, the horror movie, episode two, featuring a new zombie.

I decided that if I ever got out of bed, I was going to walk over and befriend Yvonne. I discovered, though, by hearing the nurses when they were in her room talking loudly, that she was incontinent, messed her bed daily, masturbated a lot, and slept nearly all the other hours of the day. She never left her room, of course. Nurses did go in occasionally and try to get her up but to no avail. Poor Yvonne, to be so stripped of her humanity in front of anyone who could hear the nurses. Later, I wondered what had been said and heard about me.

HIPAA (Health Insurance Portability And Accountability) regulations concerning confidentiality notwithstanding, nurses and staff talked about every patient by name in our presence. Luckily, I couldn't remember names or put faces to them. After a while though, I took notice of how they all talked about the patients by name, as did even the Administrator, who left her office door open. It was after I had become more lucid that I understood what they were saying, and about whom. I started paying attention, in case it was about me and affected my release. Little hope for that anytime soon, I discovered.

Meals were brought to my bedside for quite a while. I couldn't eat much food. It wasn't the food; it was my lack of appetite. I would take a few bites and would no longer feel hungry. I overheard the personnel discussing this and tut-tutting among themselves. I really didn't expect gourmet food, I still just wasn't hungry. I would eat a bite or two and be finished.

However, there were two bright spots in my culinary day. My favorite LPN Lawanda brought me grits one morning.

They were fabulous, and I told her so. Lawanda loved them, too. She said her mother worked there and made them. I told her to tell her mother I loved her and the grits.

After that I got a huge bowl of grits in my room each morning, covered with butter. There began to appear a sausage patty here, a piece of bacon there. This was my favorite meal, and I would finish every bite. They used this eventually to get me to sit up and eat from a tray beside the bed. I became Pavlov's human subject. The sound of the breakfast cart being wheeled into my room immediately got me trying to sit up in bed. After a while, I may have even salivated a bit!

And sometimes at night Lawanda would walk through the rooms with a tray of snacks. She would show the tray to me and ask, "What's your favorite?" I said, "Bar-B-Que potato chips." If she had one pack on her tray, she would say, "I saved it for you." She said she would save one for me whenever she could. When she didn't, she would give me a pack of M&M's, another secret treat she found I loved. She would stay and talk to me a while about her life and ask about mine. It's amazing how close I became to her. She was unfailingly kind, and when I heard her in the hall laughing or singing I felt happy. She said she loved her job. It showed.

Andrew visited me frequently to sit beside my bed and talk to me. Each time I would ask him how long it would be before I was released. My admission was for at least a month, he would say.

He told me Jude was living in my home with him but not helping out at all. Jude's daughter was coming over once in a while to help Andrew and Larisa clear things out, and bring food for Jude. He had always been a pack rat, and I had given up trying to organize his belongings. They were stacked up all over the house. Andrew said he was surprised and felt my frustration. He said as he got to know the situation he couldn't believe how much I was doing for Jude, essentially all the "activities of daily living," as they are called. When I think back, I realize it's true.

After a while I began to think of my beloved cat Squeeker,

a rescue cat, named for the sound she made instead of "Meow." She had spent most of every day either in my lap or watching me as I did activities. I loved her obsessively. Jude didn't take care of or even like her, and I began to be worried about her. Andrew said he and Larisa would feed her and keep her box cleaned out every day. I asked about her each time I saw Andrew, and he said she was fine. I still worried about her, imagining how she felt when suddenly I disappeared from her life. I felt she would be heartsick without me.

CHAPTER TWELVE: Physical Movement of a New and Different Kind

After a few days of lying in my bed all day and watching TV at night, stimulation enough for me, I was told that I would begin physical therapy soon. I was not sure I was ready to take that step, but I had no choice.

One morning right after breakfast, a smiling, tiny young girl looking about 16 years old, came into my room, removed the breakfast tray, and moved my wheelchair to the side of my bed. She told me her name, Filina, and said she would wheel me down to the physical therapy room after I got dressed. She asked me if I could get dressed by myself, but I told her I would appreciate her helping me this first time. This is how I found out what clothes Andrew brought for me. Not very many, as it turned out. It would have been enough for him, I'm sure. It really didn't matter to me. I didn't need many changes of clothing.

Filina turned out to be an experienced physical therapist who was in good shape and way stronger than she looked. She was extremely professional in her demeanor. She could sling my body parts around, I discovered. She showed me how to get out of bed and into my wheelchair. And then out of the wheelchair and back into the bed. I had no idea there was a specific technique to these things. One, two, three, four, in the right order. Then we practiced it until I could do it three times without a mistake.

This took an extraordinary amount of time as it seemed my brain and body would not work together. I kept forgetting the moves. She was patient and cheerful. Transferring from the bed to the wheelchair and back again was one of the hardest things I had to learn. It took a few days. She would let me stop after I became frustrated.

Once, I started crying as soon as she walked in the door. She looked surprised and asked why. I wailed, "I feel stupid and clumsy and can't remember what to do. I've never been like this. I'm hopeless. I'll never get better. I can't even get out of my bed and into my wheelchair!"

She said, with a kind smile, "You'll get better soon, and we'll keep practicing until you do. You're like a newborn who's learning new skills every day. You learned once, and you can do it again."

Filina's sweet encouraging attitude was exactly what I needed to persevere in this difficult situation. Feeling totally stupid and clumsy was foreign to me. I had to adjust my expectations. I wasn't going to be able to do something new the first or even second time. I had to learn patience with myself. I had to lose the perfectionist attitude I had lived with all my life. She understood this and managed to convey to me every little improvement she noted. She praised me for each move forward.

After I could get into and out of the wheelchair, Filina wheeled me to the door, turned to the right down the hall, around corners, into other halls, past the cafeteria and a living room and then to the physical therapy center. As we passed the cafeteria it looked gray and grim. Potential zombies were sitting silently around at tables. They were not talking and looked around with no facial expression.

The physical therapy program was extensive at this nursing and rehab facility. I was wheeled into a huge bright room with a high ceiling. There were about nine therapists including physical and occupational specialists. Only a few patients were there for treatment. I met Hank, who was head physical therapist of the group and Filina's boss. He was a small fit man who looked about forty. He said if I worked hard I would get better. The harder I worked, the faster I would learn, he told me. There would be no homework. I would do all the work in the physical therapy center and be there every day. Either he or Filina would be with me at all times. Filina would fetch me each morning after my breakfast, get me dressed if needed and bring me down to the fitness center, as it was familiarly called. We would work together until about lunch time or so. If I got too tired, we would rest or stop for the day.

That first day Hank extensively assessed my strength and abilities. He had me walk toward him, and he caught me as I started to fall. He gave me a walker to see how well I could use it. Not well, as it turned out. I leaned forward over the seat, slid my feet forward, stuck my butt out and moved like a snail a few feet. I felt terribly insecure. I believed I would fall.

An elderly lady came into the room at that moment and began zooming around the track in her nightdress and loose bedroom slippers. I watched her closely to try to learn something and was envious and filled with admiration. I told her on one of her swings around the track past me that she was doing great. No response, no look, nothing. She was looking straight ahead with no expression on her face. A zombie. Maybe a concentrating zombie, though? Or maybe I was invisible?

Hank helped me up and down a set of stairs with thick rails. He showed me some complicated machines and paraphernalia which I had no clue how to use. I saw bars going up and down a wall. I saw big beach balls and small colorful balls to put into holes. Of course there was a recumbent bike. There were parallel bars. Other interesting items were scattered around the area. It didn't look like any other physical therapy room I had ever seen. I liked it.

There were cheerful young adults sitting around in a kitchen area open to us. Open concept! They all introduced themselves to me, smiled and talked to me briefly. They said they might work with me occasionally. This was such a nice place that I looked forward to starting my work.

Most of the other facility staff were not like this. What a difference a cheerful, warm, and caring environment this was. It put me in a good mood. I felt a little more human and more like myself.

Several mornings later, Filina came into my room and brought the wheelchair over to my bed. By myself with her nearby, I slowly and carefully got out of bed, got dressed and then got into the wheelchair, all with her help. I told her I had not had breakfast yet. Bad mistake. She said she would take me to the cafeteria on the way to the fitness center. I was learning the *lingua franca*.

As she was wheeling me slowly down the hall, she told me to try to walk my feet as we went or slide them along in my stocking feet. (My wheelchair did not have foot attachments.) This was not possible as my feet didn't reach the floor. She had me move slightly forward in the chair with the strap holding me until they did so. She stood directly behind me to ensure my safety. We proceeded in this way down the hall and stopped at the dim cafeteria.

There were about ten tables scattered around a small room beside a curved bar. Inside the bar, people were cooking and stacking silverware and napkins. One or two patients were seated at tables but not talking. Ironically there was a game room opening off the cafeteria. I never saw anyone but staff using it. Apparently, no zombies were allowed. Occasionally, the smell of popcorn wafted out of its open door into the dining from a movie theater-size popcorn machine. I love popcorn but never had the nerve to ask if I could get some.

Filina rolled me up to a table for four with two ladies already seated there. She didn't introduce me. No comment from the two women. They did not focus on me, Filina, or the table. She said she would come back to get me after breakfast. "Oh Lordy, please don't leave me," I thought frantically, but Filina left me and proceeded down the hall. I didn't want to do this at all. Totally unsmiling silent women were to be my breakfast companions? I knew I really should attempt to converse with them out of pure courtesy.

I introduced myself and asked them their names. They said nothing and didn't look at me. I froze into silence. I had no more to give. I looked away from them.

There was a coffee machine on the counter of the bar beside my table and a stack of cups with cream and sugar. I told my silent companions I was going to get some coffee and asked if they would like a cup. For the first time, the ladies looked up in alarm, and one said, "Don't." Thinking they meant they didn't want a cup, I rolled up to the counter, poured myself a cup of coffee, and rolled back to my table, feeling proud of my accomplishment.

Suddenly, a cafeteria staff member rushed out from behind the counter and grabbed my coffee from me. "You can't get your own coffee. You have to wait for someone to take your order and then you can have it. You don't want to spill it and burn yourself," she said officiously and loudly. Though I could see her point, the way she said it reminded me of Nurse Ratched from the Jack Nicholson movie. I tried to tell her I was sorry, I was new and didn't know the rules yet, but she strutted away pompously. I shrunk into my wheelchair and looked around. I didn't need to be embarrassed. No one even noticed or looked at me. I was invisible to the patients. Oh no! Was I too a zombie?

The next thirty minutes were agony. I valiantly tried all my rusty conversational gambits on the two silent women. But there was not a sound or look from them. Finally the lady who had snatched my coffee came up to take our orders. She asked the ladies if they wanted their usual breakfast. No answer. The waitress wrote down something on her pad. Then she turned to me. "And what will you have?" I said, "Coffee," and asked what breakfast choices there were. She impatiently said, "Eggs, bacon, sausage, and toast." I said I'd have eggs, bacon and toast.

Ten minutes later she arrived with three coffees and three breakfasts. I got eggs, bacon, sausage, and toast! And at last, coffee. The two ladies had sweet rolls and their coffee. Sweet rolls? Things were getting weirder and weirder. Again I tried to say something to them but nothing other than eating was happening on their side of the table.

Finally, Filina returned to pick me up. None too soon. I exhaled and relaxed the tension in my body.

As we rolled down the hall, she asked how I had enjoyed breakfast. I said, "Not at all. It made me extremely uncomfortable that the ladies at my table were not talking to or looking at me." I begged, "May I continue to eat breakfast in my room?"

She said, "We're not ready to socialize, I see." I wanted to say that I socialized more in my room than in the cafeteria. And that I was ready, but no one else was. I held my tongue, not wanting to be seen as a smart mouth by sweet Filina. And not wanting to make waves.

So began my first day of actual PT.

It was much harder than I thought it would be. Body and mind still seemed disconnected. I was weak. But I could now understand verbal directions much better than before. Because I was still experiencing blank spaces, I don't remember everything that was done or the order of the lessons. I did notice that I was always the first one there. Later a few other patients, non-communicative and sometimes in night clothes, would come in for therapy. When I asked the fitness staff how many patients they saw per day, they said that about the same number of people came in the afternoon. That would have made a total of about twenty a day. I was assigned Hank and Filina for the entire time I was at the facility.

At the slant board, I had to lie with my head pointed down and try to lift my upper half. Notice the word "try." The wooden stairs were pretty easy if I took them slow. There were two staircase choices at the top, making a turn to the right possible or you could continue on down the other side. The handrails were very wide, so I could only touch them for balance, not actually use them as a handhold by my small hands. I was afraid of falling the first time. Walking on the wide wooden beam placed on the floor between the parallel bars was easy because you had the bars to hold on to.

I loved the beach ball exercises. For the first time I smiled. I would have my walker in front of me in the locked position and toss the ball back and forth with Filina or Hank. Later I learned to do this against the wall, and much later, without the walker. I hated having to walk around the track using the walker. I could never get comfortable with this, even when both

Hank and Filena would correct my posture over and over. Later I was to discover the reason for my problem using the walker.

The exercise where colored balls were to be placed into matching holes was timed. The order of the balls was changed for each trial. It was like "Whack-A-Mole" except the moles had to be placed in the holes by hand. There was no whacking. I found this difficult at first. Thinking, discriminating, and using quick hand-eye coordination was a lot to absorb. But I learned. And it became fun. Again, I smiled.

At the end of each session, I would use the recumbent bike. Naturally, I had to learn all the steps of getting from my wheelchair to the bike seat, adjusting the placement of the seat and setting the controls properly. This was another long learning curse, er, curve. After about two weeks, I could be trusted to do this, though Hank always stood within easy reach to stop a fall.

Then Filina would wheel me back to my room, which still seemed a complicated path with many turns down halls to either side. At first, I would again be asked to use my feet to help me move the chair forward while being pushed. One day, though, Filina asked me to hold onto the wheels, try to push them, walk my feet on the floor and move myself forward. This was extremely difficult and in fact exhausting, even for short distances. Daily she asked me to go farther down the hall. My wheelchair was large and heavy. Even with her helping me occasionally, I would get to my room and need to lie down for the rest of the day.

I was allowed to eat in my room for two meals a day. Breakfast unfortunately always began to be with the zombies in the cafeteria on the way to the fitness center. One day I saw a short attractive lady talking to a zombie. She walked normally and was smiling. When she stood up, I quickly rolled over and introduced myself. She told me her name, Emily. Alas, she could not carry on a coherent conversation and seemed afraid of me. Her eyes darted here and there. She spoke in a rapid, high pitched voice. After a few sentences, she almost ran off. I felt her anxiety acutely. I spoke to her every time I saw her but she never seemed to recognize me. She never smiled or spoke again. Another zombie.

One day in the fitness center I was stumbling awkwardly along the track in my walker, when I looked up and saw Jude sitting in a chair beside the track watching me. I didn't realize who it was at first and then did a double take and knew. I can't overstate my shock. My heart began beating faster. I immediately felt shy, defensive, clumsy and uncomfortable. I knew he was judging my progress, naturally, and wondered what he thought. I tried to smile at him, stopped and said, "Hi." He said he would wait until I finished my session and then come to the cafeteria for lunch with me. He would stay and watch the rest of my physical therapy first. "Oh no," I thought. These were pronouncements from him, not questions. I became anxious.

I had to ask Filina if this was okay and how to arrange it. Jude said he understood her answer and could handle it when we arrived at the cafeteria. I self-consciously finished my track walking and the bike under his gaze, and Jude rolled me down the hall. Filina, unfailingly helpful, came along with us. She helped us find a table and talked to the staff for us. Jude had to pay for his meal. Ha!

I listened to Jude and tried to respond normally. He wanted to talk about anything but my progress. He didn't ask me about how and what I was doing. He talked about himself, telling his usual stories about people I didn't know. He repeated these constantly to anyone who would listen. I used to listen, but now I tuned out because I knew all about Jude.

After we had finished eating, he said he would take me to my room. I asked him if he could find it. He said it was straight down the hall, the last room on the left. What? This seemed perfectly straightforward to me now, pardon the pun. Why had I been so confused? I watched carefully, and saw that he was exactly right. There were halls leading off from the main hall, but they went toward other patient rooms.

When we got to my room, I got myself onto the bed and lay down. Jude didn't offer to help me. He pulled up a chair and looked down at me. There was no smiling, no conversation.

Now he was acting like a zombie! I tried in a desultory way to talk to him but it was uncomfortable for me. It's hard to describe his totally expressionless face as he loomed above my bed. He actually had nothing to say, so I became silent and fell into a doze. When I awoke, he was still there but said he had to leave. He said he would visit again. I hoped he wouldn't.

And he didn't.

Jude's visit depressed me. It looked like our previous relationship was really over. I would be alone. I thought about Jude and realized that as a psychiatrist, he had been paid to listen to people and maybe was tired of it. Before my illness, he had talked all the time to me, but he also listened to me. There was back and forth conversation. I always listened intently, learning everything I could from him as I believed him to be intelligent and articulate. I talked avidly with him and he listened to me then. But now, he saw me as demented. There would be no conversation between us.

I went into a funk. I tried to call Andrew but still hadn't mastered the cell phone. So I lay in my room until Lawanda came in with my dinner. She said I seemed quiet. I told her I was feeling down after my partner visited me, and things were not good with us. She commiserated and told me one funny outlandish story after another about her no-good ex-boyfriend. She had me laughing with her until we both cried. She was a perfect person to work with anxious or depressed patients. What a lovely, helpful lady.

Later that night, Andrew came to see me, and I told him about Jude's visit. He knew about it already. He asked me how I felt about Jude. I said I wasn't sure. I wanted to get better before I decided. Inside, I think I already knew.

I also asked Andrew to show me again how to use the cell phone. He found the cord was missing, and it had lost its charge! He went out and told the nurse to bring another cord, which she did. We were going to have to wait for the new charge, so Andrew said he would come back the next day. He did so and tried to show me how to use the phone. I forgot as soon as he left.

I later discovered that Andrew, every day, was having to drive to my house, do cleaning and sorting there, take things to Goodwill or advertise on the internet to sell them, drive around looking for a chef's job, drive to see me and talk with staff, and find time to spend with Larisa. Every day! He and Larisa even came by a few times and took me out to lunch. It was a long drive from the other side of town to where I was staying. He also was trying to socialize with Jude, who was mostly watching TV and eating food Andrew or Jude's daughter cooked.

Andrew never once complained and still has never done so.

CHAPTER THIRTEEN: Weirder and Weirder

Between therapies and meals, I would lie on my bed, dozing or watching television or doing nothing. It was restful.

One afternoon, a dark-haired woman in her forties came into my room and said she was my psychiatrist. She wanted to talk with me about my illness. She sat down beside my bed, leaned toward me eagerly, and asked me to tell her all about what happened to me from the beginning. I started with the fall and proceeded through all the rest. She smiled at me throughout and looked me in the eyes. She asked how I felt things were going. She seemed very sympathetic. I liked her.

And then she became very animated, her eyes gleamed, and she said that the exact same fall had happened to her in the very same place where it happened to me. Every detail including a lady helping her, her husband not taking her to the emergency room and her subsequent loss of walking and mental faculties! She said that after therapy, she had gained back all her faculties and had been able to return to her practice.

I was flabbergasted. I said, "You're kidding me, right?"

"No, I swear," she said.

I kept telling her, "I can't believe it." She got ready to leave. She smiled and said she would see me soon.

I never saw her again.

I never asked anyone about her. No staff asked me about her visit. I thought maybe this was a counseling technique I was unaware of, used to reassure me and give me hope for recovery. Or it was a test of my cognitive skills. However, her strange story did not reassure me. I was conflicted as to whether to believe her or not. I have thought about this since and think she may have been a little crazy—maybe even a talking zombie. A weird incident like this would unnerve me for days.

Next a very tall man came to see me who said he was an occupational therapist who would visit me once a week. As I lay in the bed, he stood over me with a clipboard. He was an insufferable person who talked the entire time about himself. I ended up counseling him about his wayward daughter and willful wife. It would exhaust me to try to get a word in edgewise. He, also, never returned. I like to think, though, that I helped him. He called me at home several times after I was discharged. When I saw his name on the telephone, I would not answer, and finally blocked his number.

These two experiences led to a setback in my mental state. I felt like I must be going crazy or they were. I don't know why I didn't ask anyone about it. I had a case of passive acceptance. I didn't take the time to evaluate deeply what happened to me. This fact makes me think that my brain was resting from its trauma. I've read that brain injury victims need a restful quiet time to aid the brain's recovery process.

I now believe these two people were in training at best. It was exhausting trying to interact politely with such unprofessional people. I may have been without all my faculties, but I knew when something was not normal. I sometimes imagined that two mental patients had escaped and come to my room. Anything was possible since my room was beside an outside door that was "always" locked. And there was a gate in the fence between the two buildings, again "always" locked.

There are mysteries about my stay at the rehab center that will never be solved. I'm letting them remain so. "Water under the bridge."

Chapter Fourteen: More Therapies

A real occupational therapist (OT), Melanie, began visiting me and was truly helpful. She was young, cheerful, confident, and had just had a baby, whom we talked a little about during our first session. I found her relaxing. The first day, she played the game called Patience, I think, where you turn over cards one at a time, turn them back over, and try to find the first one for a match. She was my opponent and destroyed me. She said she practiced a lot.

She had me describe activities people in pictures were doing. She asked me to fold a towel. She showed me a calendar and asked me what day of the week it was (no idea) and what my schedule was today. She said she would get me a calendar which I would fill out daily, and we would discuss. She had a book for me to fill in all about my family and our history. She said she would see me two days a week in the afternoon.

On her next visit, she brought the calendar, and showed me how she wanted me to use it. We started by looking at the day and date, putting in her schedule, then PT, meals, and finally Andrew's usual visits. She wanted me to make corrections if plans changed. Believe it or not, this was hard for me to keep up with and use in the beginning. She would visit and ask me the day of the week, and I could not tell her. I had forgotten to use the calendar. Patiently she would go over it again. Then at the end of the visit, she would ask again about the day and date. We would talk about my entries (at first none) and what I had done during those times. She would ask me about the next day's plans.

Little by little, I began to think about such things. She went over my family history with me and asked questions about each person, such as birthdays, birthplace, role in the family, etc. It would have been nice if I had asked Andrew to bring pictures to me, but I didn't think of it and neither did he.

I finally learned how to use the cell phone! Melanie taught me after many repetitions. She told me a trick her father taught her how to navigate around the phone. We made phone calls. My phone was already programmed with phone numbers, once I found them.

One day Melanie had me make an appointment to see her in the fitness room in two days at a certain time. We put it on the calendar. I was to make my way down there in my wheelchair or walker. At the scheduled time, I got up, retrieved my walker and went to the door to my room. I opened the door and carefully began making my way down the hall. One of the physical therapists I recognized just "happened" to be walking the other way and asked where I was headed. I told him I had an appointment to see my OT Melanie in the fitness room. I had that down pat. He said he was going that way, turned around (!), and said he would walk with me. How comforting and discreet that kindness was to me on my first trip alone.

My PT and OT continued throughout the next weeks. I still had trouble using the walker and rolling the wheelchair down the hall by myself. Most of the time Filina came to get me, or other staff saw me struggling down the hall and would come to my assistance. In PT I was beginning go outside and throw the ball around with other patients. These patients seemed better off than the other ones I had seen. They actually smiled but didn't talk to each other. Or to me. But it was cheerful outside.

My therapies seemed to be going well. I could get in and out of bed, dress, walk to the bathroom with my walker, make my way around my room, and sit in an armchair for a while. I could transfer into and out of my wheelchair. The walker over distances was still not possible for me, and I never attempted a trip alone in the wheelchair. Staff had to accompany me when I wanted a shower. That was the rule.

Suddenly, though, I began to have a few "falls" in my room, which I denied were falls. But thinking back on them, I guess they were. I had become overconfident. Several times when I was getting into or out of bed, I would be unable to reach the floor and would slide down onto it. It was slow and didn't hurt me.

I would try to get off the floor and back into bed but could not do so. I tried reaching up and pulling on the fitted sheet to no avail. Tried using the potty chair to pull up, using the bars under the bed, tried turning around every way I could imagine would help. My arms weren't strong enough. I would end up exhausted, tangled up in sheets and clothing, and panting. I saw myself flopping around like a fish out of water, an image which struck me as funny. But I dreaded the moment a nurse would find me. This would be considered a setback and delay my release.

Inevitably, a nurse would come in and find me calmly lying on the floor somewhere near my bed, saying cheerfully, "I didn't fall, I just slid trying to get out of bed. I'm not hurt."

They said firmly, "That's a fall. You could have been hurt!" Another staff member would be sent for, and together they examined me and got me up into bed. They told me I had to use the call button if I wanted to get out of bed. I now know this was for my safety but I chafed at the restriction.

I soon realized, though, that the nurses were so busy that my buzzer summons would probably go unanswered one day, and it did. At that time, I tried again unsuccessfully to get out of and back into bed. And, the next day, again. There were more lectures. I was stubbornly trying to be more independent. The day I succeeded in getting out of bed by myself and back into it safely was a red-letter day for me, a milestone of huge proportions. Now I could use my walker to get to my own bathroom instead of having to use the bedside potty. I wish someone had taught me how to do this. As it was, I taught myself.

As I got better, I had an insatiable desire to know everything that was going on around me.

There were isolated bright spots among the staff. Every few days a large friendly man, Larry, would come to my room in the afternoon and mop my floor. He smiled, sang and laughed the whole time. He talked to me, asked about my family, what

I had done for a living, and what music I liked. He had a great baritone voice, and we sometimes sang hymns together, ones we both knew. He told me about his family and his church. He was the happiest man I saw there. And he had to do just as much work as any of the other staff. His line was, "I can't complain." I still think of Larry as a fine example of a Godly man.

CHAPTER FIFTEEN: How Can I Get Out of Here

During Andrew's visits, I began to ask him when I could go home. I longed to sit on my front porch, look out at the trees, have a cup of coffee and listen to the birds singing. I wanted to lounge in my own living room, eat in my dining room, sleep in my bedroom. I wanted to walk the familiar floors of my home and go back to my old life. I didn't realize this wouldn't be possible with my current capabilities. I would not be able to live independently. Arrangements would have to be made.

Andrew talked to me about it honestly. He calmly said I needed someone to stay with me all day for a while and help me with activities of daily living. I hadn't thought about that. We also needed to have a home visit from Filina and Hank. They were to ascertain if I could get from a car into my home by myself. They would also examine the inside of my house for safety issues.

I needed to have a physical therapist and occupational therapist come to my home to work with me there. Andrew said he was working on getting all this set up.

I asked about Jude and whether he would be there to watch me during the day. Andrew asked me if I wanted him to ask Jude that question. We agreed we should at least ask how he felt about it. I was unsure, though it would solve a lot of immediate problems. Home Health Care Agencies were also being consulted.

Andrew called me the next day. He said Jude didn't want to take care of me, even to the extent of sitting beside my bed part of the day. I was devastated but not surprised. Andrew asked me what I wanted to do. I said I would like to think about it for a while.

I thought long and hard about Jude and decided I no longer wanted to be involved with him or live with him. I couldn't

69

cook and clean for him, and he didn't want to help me at all. I told Andrew my decision. He said I would have to tell Jude. He didn't feel it was his place to do so. I asked him to have Jude call me.

Jude called me the next day.

Without mincing words, I said immediately, "Jude, I'm sorry but I want you to move out of my house as soon as possible. I want you to be gone before I come home."

"When are you coming home?" he asked.

"Within a few weeks," I said.

"Why do you want me to leave?" he asked anxiously. "I don't want to." There were no words about love or devotion.

I explained, unnecessarily I thought, "You've told Andrew that you won't care for or stay with me to be sure I'm safe. This hurts me terribly. Do you expect me to continue to live with you under these circumstances? Do you think I could continue to take care of you? Also, you've done nothing to help Andrew sort our belongings or move his furniture in. You're sitting in a chair watching television all day and letting others wait on you. They even have to bring you your meals. You haven't asked if you can do anything to help Andrew or me. You haven't once asked me how I'm feeling or given me hope for my future. You've visited me only once in the rehab center. I don't need or want you in my life. I'm sorry if this makes you feel bad, but I actually wonder why you haven't left already. I don't feel love from you. I'm saying goodbye to you Jude," I said firmly. I was shaking but he didn't have to know that.

"But where will I go?" he asked plaintively. Still thinking only of himself! He could have at least asked me to change my mind! Or said that he would change.

I resisted the impulse to tell him, "That's not my problem," but firmly said instead, "You have family locally and your sister has a large house in Maine. I'm sure they'll help you make plans. You don't need to contact me again. I'd prefer you didn't. Just be sure you and your belongings are gone when I return home. Andrew can let you know when that'll be."

That night I received a call from Trevor, Jude's son. He said frantically, "Please let my dad stay with you. No one in the family wants to live with him. No one. He has nowhere to go." I couldn't believe he had said this to me. I told him, "No," and explained (unnecessarily I thought) why not in detail. I then said, "Why can't you help him find a place to live? He's a grown man. He can support himself." He continued to beg me. When Trevor realized my mind was made up, he began to get nasty. He told me I owed it to Jude. "No, I don't. I have taken care of him as long as I can or want to," I retorted. "And he isn't willing to help care for me now." I then told him my physical therapist had arrived and I had to hang up—and did. I was shaking again.

Hallelujah, I had done the right thing, I knew. The deed was done. I called Andrew and told him about the conversation. He was supportive and wanted to know if I was all right.

Chapter Sixteen: My Family Visits

Soon after this took place, I had unexpected visitors. One of my younger brothers Jim and his wife Elaine, who live in a nearby town, came to see me and asked if I wanted them to bring me anything the next time they came. They probably meant clothes or books. I said, "Bar-B-Que chips and M&M's"! I craved junk food. They looked surprised and then laughed and said they would bring some on their next visit. And they did.

Jim said he was going to speak to Andrew about what steps he (Andrew) should be taking. I said I thought he was taking appropriate steps on his own but suggested that Jim could ask to see if he needed any assistance.

Jim began talking about the minutiae of his life. I'm sure he did so out of nervousness. Jim is a retired Air Force captain and is used to command. He usually dominates a room. I still remember him as a darling little boy following me everywhere, and I feel tender toward him when I do. There have been times in past when we were very close. The room got noisy. Jim speaks very loudly. I got tired. When she could get a word in edgewise, his wife kindly asked how I was doing, but I began to feel anxious having been used to peace and quiet.

After a mercifully short visit, where I wasn't saying much since they were doing all the talking, they left. Their visit left me frazzled and anxious. Not good for me. But I'm also sure it was stressful for them since this was the first time they had seen me since my diagnosis.

A few days later Jim asked Andrew to meet him for breakfast. Jim provided him with a list of things to do. He went over the list with Andrew and asked what had been done. Politely Andrew went over each item, showed Jim that all was currently in process and thanked him for his effort on my behalf. I'm sure out of love for me Jim needed to make sure that everything was being taken care by my son. I'm afraid he underestimated how capable Andrew is and Andrew knew it. Another family visit took place shortly after. This time, my sister Elizabeth, a nurse, and her husband John, a retired Air Force Colonel; Jim and Elaine, and my brother David, a yacht broker and sailor visited. They began having quite the family reunion at the other end of the room. I'm not sure they even greeted me. I think they were all uncomfortable with me and not sure how to act. I couldn't keep up with their conversation and spaced out totally. Jim, Elizabeth and John were laughing more and more loudly and talking faster and faster as they usually do, telling jokes which I ordinarily find amusing. My sister then seemed to get hysterical talking about me. She began to cry loudly. It frightened me.

David, the middle of five siblings, was quiet. I could feel his oasis of calm from across the room. In a little while, he brought a chair over to the side of my bed opposite to the unruly crowd and sat down. He quietly asked how I was doing. He looked me in the eye and listened to my answer. He asked a number of quiet questions. He expressed sorrow this had happened to me, but said he was confident I was going to be okay soon.

David said he knew me, and this wasn't going to keep me down. He said he thought I was better already, from what he had heard. He was impressed at all the therapy I was getting. He sat silently, allowing me to rest my jangled nerves. He asked if the noise was bothering me. When I said it was, he said it bothered him too, and he figured it would be upsetting me. He said he loved me and not to worry. I asked him about himself and his wife Leigh, and he answered briefly. He soothed me. His visit helped me calm down.

Finally, my family decided to continue their visit at a restaurant down the street before returning to their hotels. Bidding me good-by, they left. Not one of them had even talked to or asked about me. They were probably nervous to be around me. I had Alzheimer's, and they had no idea what to say to me. Was I a zombie to them?

Comforting brother David stayed on a while. Later, I told him how much his quiet conversation that night had meant to me. He said he learned during his heart surgeries how upsetting a noisy family visit can be. He said he was looking at me all alone amid the chaos, and he empathized totally. So he came over to help me. I felt more like myself afterwards.

Chapter Seventeen: Going Home

Andrew consulted with the nursing home administrator and met with all my therapists and staff. They decided I could go home when I could use my walker better and demonstrate my ability to balance without it. I would also have to demonstrate I could walk alone across the backyard and my patio, and up the three stairs to my back door without my walker. They were confident by now I could do it, but they didn't realize the yard was large and the ground was uneven and hilly. They were picturing a small flat backyard.

Hank and Filina would be nearby in case I should start to fall. Everyone felt it would be important for me to be able to independently get across my back yard to and from my automobile. No one was aware at that time that Dr. Medzul would not allow me to drive. None of my therapists thought of me as an Alzheimer's patient by this time. They were concentrating on my balance and mobility while walking.

Since Andrew still had things to finalize at the house, and he was working now six days a week as a chef at a new restaurant in town, a firm date needed to be set for the test. We put two weeks on my calendar.

I looked at the calendar every day. I was filled with joy and hope. However, in my enthusiasm to move home, I would get the days confused. Each time Andrew would visit me, I would say something like, "Only two more days until my test"!

He would pull out the calendar and kindly show me I was on the wrong day of the week. This happened several times. I was still not cognitively well, though physically I had improved a great deal.

Once, I told the nurses, "Today is moving day," and I packed up my few belongings. They didn't check with administration, and I waited in my room all day. Andrew didn't arrive. I asked a nurse to help me call him on my cell phone.

Andrew patiently told me that the test had to be completed before I could come home. I couldn't go home without being able to walk in my yard. It seemed to be some kind of legal issue. The test would be the during the coming week. Oh well, that was not too far off, we said. Actually, I felt like I wanted to cry. I swallowed my disappointment and put my things away, looking ahead to the following week for my test.

Filina and Hank upped my training to work exclusively on moving and balancing without my walker. I improved. Hank and Filina were convinced I could do well. On the test date, Andrew took the morning off from work. He drove me up the alley behind my house, followed by Hank and Filina. I was nervous. So were Andrew and the therapists, since no one was allowed to accompany me. There were no rails to hold on to.

We all took a deep breath. Filina and Hank took positions in yard and I started down the broad brick stairs to the first level of the backyard. I vividly remember the shadows the trees made on the steps and ground. I was afraid every minute I would fall but was determined not to do so. I moved slowly with my arms out to the sides like a tightrope walker. I made it!

The next stage was going to be harder. The ground was grassy and uneven. Hank and Filina kept close to either side of me. Believe me I walked *very* slowly and carefully to the next flight of stairs. These stairs were made of wide flat stones and were relatively easy to manage. The final level was an uneven brick patio that I had made years ago and knew well. A piece of cake.

That test was over. They said I had passed! By not falling.

Andrew carried the folded wheelchair up the three wooden steps to the back door, through the door to the kitchen, unfolded the wheelchair, and locked the wheels. He then helped me up the stairs. After all my training I easily got into the chair! Andrew rolled me through the dining room, the living room, past the bathroom and into my bedroom. There was a hospital bed set up and a potty chair beside my bed.

The therapists approved of the arrangements. They made a

few suggestions to move objects in the house I could trip on. Then they said cheerfully, "See you back at rehab!" I was elated. I gleefully thanked them and hugged Andrew.

Since Andrew had to return to work, we talked briefly, and he drove me back with the wheelchair to the rehab facility and rolled me to my room, both of us smiling widely.

My happiness was complete. This was my last obstacle to returning home!

Andrew still had to schedule the physical and occupational home therapy visits through either a public home health agency or a private group he had researched. Their expenses were mostly covered by my health insurance and Medicare. Visits were scheduled for soon after I moved back home.

The next weekend I was allowed to go home. I sat in the wheelchair and Andrew stacked my belongings on my lap. We discovered we had to visit all my therapists and staff to get them to sign off on a checklist before we could leave. The last person to sign off was the administrator. This took a while. Then I was wheeled to the fitness room for a final good-bye. But sadly no one was there.

When Andrew took me to the lobby, there was a huge crowd of staff and patients, including all the therapists! They clapped, smiled and cheered for me as I was wheeled through. Even the zombies were there! I became emotional, laughing and crying at the same time. It was a wonderful way to end my stay and meant the world to me. Even Andrew was affected. I tear up as I write this.

I forgot my painful moments. *I was going home!*

When we arrived, Larisa was there to help welcome me and get me settled. During my absence, Andrew had moved himself and most of their furniture out of their apartment down the street and into the large upstairs area of my home where they would stay until other arrangements could be made. Larisa was staying in the apartment for a few days to finish packing and cleaning before joining us.

Everything in my home was spotless. When I came to my room, I was greeted with bright pink sheets on my hospital bed.

They were new and beautiful. Larisa said Andrew picked them out. The color lit up the room. I still remember how the room glowed in the afternoon light, making me happy. A colorful spread was folded at the bottom of the bed. I loved it. I was essentially in my familiar bedroom from upstairs except with a better view out two sides of the room. I was relieved that we had a hospital bed, which was much easier to get in and out of than my former queen bed. Andrew showed me how to lower and raise the rails and use the various other controls. I loved being able to raise the head of the bed! This was the one control I could remember!

All my furniture had been moved downstairs to my new bedroom. My dresser, lamps and end tables had been moved, with their contents intact. All my clothes had been hung in my closet. Most of my books had been moved into the extensive bookcases lining one wall of my new bedroom. A TV was set up in a corner which I could watch from my bed.

A potty chair was beside my bed. My walker was there, too when I was ready to move around. I was to take a shower while sitting in the tub. Andrew had purchased a tub bench extending from the outside to the inside of the tub, which he said a therapist would train me to use.

Andrew had also provided me with a personal alarm device to wear around my neck in case of a fall or other emergency. It would alert him and emergency personnel to come to the house to take care of me. It was on my bedside table when I wasn't moving around the house. He said he would teach me how to use it later.

The three of us went out on the front porch and sat talking quietly, gazing at the sunset. Andrew and Larisa had a small glass of wine to celebrate while I had a sip "just to be neighborly." It was the perfect ending to a perfect day. I already felt better. I knew exactly where I was!

Andrew and Larisa helped me into bed when I said I was tired. They went to the kitchen to prepare dinner for us. They later served mine to me on a tray in my bed. I was totally pampered and made to feel important. I smile when I think of it.

What a wonderful and loving homecoming they gave me. I couldn't thank them enough. I will never fathom how the two of them managed to do all the things they accomplished in such a short time. They are extraordinary! And hard workers. They moved their belongings twice, prepared my home for me, cleaned and cleared out years of unused items, moved furniture, arranged treatments for me, Andrew visited almost every day and reassured me, and they adapted to my new mental and physical conditions. They thought about and acted on my needs and made sure that Jude and his mountains of stuff had moved out of the house. No easy task and they did it all on their own.

Jude had been offered a place to live with his son Trevor in Raleigh, North Carolina. This was to be temporary, for three months. Then Jude's daughter close by in Greensboro would take over for three months. They hoped by then they could find Jude a place to live on his own.

When Andrew showed me how he had arranged the downstairs of my house, I was totally relieved to see he had cleared out the room Jude had used as an office. It was now a lovely, immaculate den. I could feel my stomach relax as I walked in. The reader can only imagine the former state of this room, dirty dishes, papers everywhere, computer equipment stacked up willy-nilly, discs scattered over everything, the floor covered with computer magazines, and the overall look of a hoarder's space. I had refused to enter it at some point in the past. It jangled my nerves. It made me think Jude was seriously disturbed. I couldn't reconcile this room with my view of who he was. My complaints had fallen on deaf ears. He said I was "anal and obsessive-compulsive" and just ignored my wishes. I learned to ignore the room. I learned later he himself was obsessive-compulsive, hence the hoarding, I suppose.

Dr. Medzul met with Andrew and me in his office a few days after I arrived home. It was now the first week of August 2018, He wanted to assess my progress. He gave me an abbreviated form of the cognitive tests ("T" instead of "F" words this time, thank heavens) and physical tests he had performed earlier. I could walk backward and forwards slowly, as well as turn around. My physical skills were better, my cognitive not so much.

He said with certainty, "Well, you do have Alzheimer's Disease."

He didn't know how quickly it would progress. He said he wanted me to join his long-term national study, which would give us continuing results of my condition. I would have scans, bloodwork, cognitive and physical tests periodically. Andrew and I agreed. He said he would personally follow up with me frequently during the study. This turned out not to be true. We left his office comforting each other that I would be okay, in spite of what Dr. Medzul had said. Andrew and I couldn't help thinking I would get better. Apparently Dr. Medzul did not.

CHAPTER EIGHTEEN: Home Therapists

My first home therapist upon my returning home was a physical therapist from a home health agency on August 9, 2018. He made two visits in the next four days. Andrew had requested this service after my discharge from the nursing facility at the end of July.

The therapist was not a good one. He assessed me only briefly. He did his paperwork at a snail's pace. He handed me a thick folder of exercises to do with no instructions as to which ones to do, how many repetitions and how to do them. He filled out paperwork as I tried to do them. On his second visit, he never checked my progress but gave me new pages of exercises. There was no apparent connection to the previous ones. Andrew complained and he was dismissed. We decided not to use that agency.

Instead Andrew contracted with a private agency, Bayada, he had researched. All the therapists there had doctorates and were certified professionals. They came highly recommended.

A Dr. Arul met Andrew and me in my living room on September 10. Andrew stayed to watch the first session so he would be prepared to help me practice. After learning that I had a terrible fear of falling, Dr. Arul attached a wide belt around my waist, buckled it and held on to it. By having me then try to fall, he demonstrated how he could stop me with the safety belt. He then had Andrew hold the strap. No problem! I was not afraid of falling with someone holding the belt after that. This therapist immediately gained my confidence.

He assessed my skills on the walker, getting out of an easy chair holding and not holding on to the arms, and doing half pushups from the back of the chair. He asked, "Can you get up off the floor by yourself?"

"No. I'm glad you asked. I really want to learn how!" I told him about how impossible I had found it to get up from the floor in the rehabilitation facility. I had laughed at myself about it but was serious about that never happening again. He assured me it was easy to learn, and he would teach me on his next visit. I wanted to hug him!

Since my arms and legs were strong enough to get up from the chair and without holding on to help myself, he told me he would teach me how to use my walker properly and eventually walk without it.

Then he asked if I wanted to learn to walk up and down the three flights of steep granite steps in front of my house. Astonished, I said "Yes!" Once I could get down to the sidewalk, he told me, I would use my walker to walk up to the corner and back again— about a thousand feet. Finally, he said, I would make it to the corner and back *without the walker!*

I wouldn't fall, Dr. Arul assured me, because I would be fully ready before we tried it, and he would be there beside me every step of the way.

And those were the ambitious goals Dr. Arul thought I could achieve. And soon! I could hardly believe I would be able to learn to do all the things he outlined. I was full of hope and excitement about his plan. I told him I would do the best I could and vowed to myself I would succeed no matter how hard I would have to work. As they say in real estate, I was a "motivated buyer."

Dr. Arul told me he noticed immediately the walker was not adjusted properly for me. No one at the rehab facility had noticed that before! He adjusted the handles to make them lower, and I could finally use it correctly. I practiced walking from room to room in my home for the rest of the session. He worked on my posture to correct my protruding derriere. I was to place my abdomen close to the seat of the walker and stand up straight.

The bad habit I had learned previously was hard to unlearn. It took Andrew smilingly reminding me every time he saw me using the walker to "move in closer and stand up straight, Mom. Don't stick your butt out."

Next Dr. Arul said there was no need to wait for the next class. He taught me how to get up from the floor. This is a useful skill for anyone to master, I think. From lying on my back on the floor, I had to roll over and get up on my hands and knees. Then I had to crawl to the nearest chair or other non-movable object and bend over it, placing my arms across the seat. At that point, I would push up and forward with my legs to lean over the seat of the chair. After rising up on my elbows, I would hold on the arms of the chair (if no arms, the back or sides of the seat), and stand up, using the chair to support some of my weight. It worked every time. I was thrilled to know how to do this. I didn't have to be afraid of being abandoned on the floor if no one was around. It gave me more confidence to try walking around the house. It's a skill I have found to be useful in a number of ways. Now when I have to get down on my knees to do something, I use this technique to get up. I can also lock my walker wheels and get up holding on to it!

This was definitely a satisfying and fruitful visit. Andrew and I were both more than pleased with Dr. Arul. We felt optimistic.

CHAPTER NINETEEN: A Bad Penny Returns

After this first therapy visit, I had an unwelcome visitor. Jude had begged Andrew to let him come with his son Phillip to move a few more of his things from our basement. He also wanted to see me.

Andrew asked me how I felt about the request. I'm sure I must have sighed. "As long as you'll be in the next room. I might as well get this over with."

The next day Jude and his son came over. Phillip greeted me, packed Jude's belongings, along with some of my classical music CD's, unfortunately, and then stayed in the kitchen talking with Andrew.

Jude sat with me in the living room. I was uncomfortable, wondering what he would say. Taking one look at me, he started crying. I had no reaction. It's sad but true how I had become desensitized to Jude's crying.

I apparently had lost a lot of weight, and Jude mentioned it after drying his tears. I just said, "Oh." I noticed he had, too, but didn't mention it.

Jude started sobbing loudly again and began pacing the room.

He said, "Please take me back. I'll do anything you want. I'll take care of you. I'll give you your medicine. I'll help you exercise. I'll cook for you, even. You won't have to lift a finger."

I just couldn't put any credence in his promises anymore. I said quietly, "I'm sorry I just can't believe you'll follow through on what you're saying." Then I sat silently. Like Mary Poppins I thought, "Promises are like piecrusts—easily made and easily broken."

He continued crying throughout this speech. He then came and sat beside me again. He said, "I think about you all the time."

I blurted out, "I'm sorry. I don't think about you at all." Pretty cruel of me, I think now, but I was saying what I meant. He was not on my radar anymore. But I could have phrased it in a kinder way. I was extremely angry at him. At that he really began sobbing loudly. I was used to this and thought about the fact that he had not once inquired about how I was doing. It was all about him as usual. I stayed calm. Finally, he quieted down and sat beside me. At this point, I reached over and put my hand over his and said, "I'm sorry, Jude, I just don't feel anything for you any longer. It's time for you to go."

I held on to his arm and walked with him into the kitchen and said good-by. Andrew then supported me to my bedroom. It was really over. I was relieved.

As it turned out, it was not over yet. It would take him more than six months to remove all his belongings. However, I made sure to be away when he came to my house.

Chapter Twenty: Physical Therapy Progresses Quickly

Now that I could use my walker and get up from the floor, it was time to learn to walk safely through the house on my own. Every day I practiced diligently until I felt comfortable moving from place to place.

On his next visit Dr. Arul put the strap around my waist and had me walk a few steps without my walker. I screwed up my courage and tentatively took a few steps. He showed me how to keep my feet apart to balance myself more safely. This was a big help. I successfully walked a short while around the house. I can't adequately express how absolutely stupendous that made me feel. I was on my own, on my own two feet, walking! Dr. Arul then asked Andrew and Larisa, who were bystanders, to walk with me often in the house, with and without the walker, but using the strap. They later did this religiously. By this, I mean we were all praying that I wouldn't fall!

Next Dr. Arul demonstrated how to look for and lean on pieces of furniture or the sides of door frames while walking around the house without the strap. This would help me maintain my balance and increase my feeling of security. It was actually easier than using the walker so I began to practice it frequently. At first Andrew or Larisa stood watch over me, but they and I gradually I gained confidence little by little, day by day. Even though I had made it through the backyard once earlier during my test, I had been running on pure adrenaline and nerve. I had to learn to walk calmly and deliberately, heel-toe, heel-toe. I had to keep looking at the floor and concentrate on placement of my feet. At the suggestion of Dr. Arul I began counting my steps instead of thinking of my fear.

On this second visit he gave me a sheet of leg and foot exercises, showed me how to do them, and then observed me to be sure I did them correctly. He said, "Do these every day, ten repetitions each. If you feel up to it, do them two or three times a day." I did these faithfully and still do today. They slowly strengthened my legs, ankles and feet, and have kept my hips limber. My cores muscles were part of these exercises. As I mentioned before, I was starting from zero on core muscles!

On his third visit, Dr. Arul was in the living room with me when he asked out of the blue, "Are you ready to try going up and down the granite stairs in front of your house"?

Good grief! I hesitated and timidly said, "I think so." Actually, I was really afraid, but I thought I should try it now or never. I started shaking.

Dr. Arul noticed and said, "Don't worry. I won't let you fall. I'll teach you how to safely go up and down those stairs. I guarantee you'll soon conquer your fear of them. We're going to watch for any rough places on the steps and learn to avoid them. You'll be looking down at what's in front of you before you take a step. We'll take all the time you need. I believe you can do this"!

Hearing him say this, I put my trust in him. It occurred to me that if I fell, he would really get in trouble!

We exited my living room and went onto the porch. Dr. Arul put my strap around me. There were railings down either side of the first set of steps. I was to hold on to one of the handrails with both hands and step slightly sideways down the stairs, like a crab. He asked me to step down with my strongest leg, bringing the other leg down beside it. Works every time for me. Some days one leg feels stronger than usual and I switch the process. That works well for me, too.

After the first set of steps down, however, I had to free-walk over a level concrete portion to the next railing at the top of two flights of stairs. Dr. Arul held me with the strap, and I shakily walked over and almost dived for the one railing in the middle of the stairs. This really did frighten me. He made me practice it back and forth for what seemed like forever. I couldn't imagine ever doing it without someone holding on to me. I could see down the two flights of steps and imagine myself falling down, down, down them. I shook away that image. Too frightening!

"That's enough for today," he kindly said. Andrew and Larisa were to practice this with me often.

To this day, I'm still slightly nervous walking over to that rail alone. I concentrate, counting my steps, with a residual fear about falling down the stairs to the sidewalk. The good part is that it makes me *very* careful.

On the next visit, after accompanying me down the scary and steep remaining two flights of stairs with my strap firmly in his hand, Dr. Arul left me on the sidewalk. He climbed up to the porch to retrieve and carry my walker down the stairs to me. Again, he pointed out that I needed to become confident that I could walk to the corner on the uneven concrete pavement. He assured me he would teach me how to do it. We would take all the time we needed.

We then proceeded, turning left down the sidewalk. This was the most uneven section of the pavement. I had to watch carefully to be sure there were no raised places in the concrete. After trying this quite a few times, I was able to make it to the corner and back using the walker with Dr. Arul holding me with the strap. I felt a wonderful surge of pride, magnified by the praise I received. I love praise!

On his next visit, I had to learn to use the walker without his holding onto me with his strap and walk to the corner and back. He stayed beside me, and I knew he wouldn't let me fall. Walking without the strap was accomplished on the first try. My confidence was growing with each new task. And there was much practicing between visits.

The last phase of my training was to get down the stairs on my own holding on to the rails, with no strap, with him beside me, carrying my walker. Then I was to proceed to the end of the block with the walker nearby but without holding on to it. Dr. Arul stayed by my side, but I was afraid at first. We proceeded up to the corner and back, a distance of a thousand feet. I was allowed to stop and lean on trees, telephone poles or nearby stone walls.

I finally was able to do this, albeit slowly and precariously. I felt rickety when I walked on the sidewalk. When I was tired Dr. Arul would take a break, put the strap around me or move the walker in front of me. We practiced this trip for a few more visits, and Dr. Arul instructed Andrew and Larisa to practice this with me. They did so every day. I became stronger and improved with daily practice. Dr. Arul told us that I didn't have to be perfect at this, just know how to balance and walk. The distance and strength would come with practice.

With all of his wonderful goals for me completed toward the end of September, Dr. Arul signed off on my therapy. I was on my own! It had taken just three weeks. He said I was amazing. I just smiled and smiled. Suddenly, I looked forward to each new day.

Daily, I practiced the skills and exercises I had learned. I built up my distance without the walker little by little over the next year and a half. I have even succeeded in walking downhill. I purchased a cane just in case I need to get my balance and to keep from speeding up going downhill, something I tend to do.

I can now walk around the block including up- and downhill. I can also walk through a large store without the cane. Level floors are easy for me.

I never use my walker anymore, I say proudly. It still amazes me how far I've come! Even though progress has come with ups and downs, I'm still steadily moving forward.

Now I am able to walk from my car in the driveway, through my backyard, and into my backdoor with no support. Carrying groceries, garbage or recycling! I can do the same with groceries up and down my front stairs using the rails. I think of it as good exercise.

I feel gratitude for God's help. My faith has strengthened every day through prayer and reflection. I've thought of all the ways God literally saved my life. It makes me amazed and happy that, unworthy as I am, I am His beloved. He granted me a miracle. And put Andrew and Larisa by my side.

A week or so before Dr. Arul finished his therapy, an

occupational therapist from his agency, Dr. Perry, made her first visit. She presented herself professionally. She asked me what skills I wanted to learn. I told her, "Getting in and out of my bed and the bathtub, using my bedside potty, and getting my Depends on and off from a standing or sitting position." She said she would help me as well with other problems she observed as we went along.

She gave me a latex strap. I already had dumbbells. She demonstrated arm exercises using these devices, watched me do them, and gave me one page of them, including instructions and pictures. She demonstrated them and made sure I could do them. She told me that was enough for one day. I had known she would tell me to practice them every day. She did. That was a given.

The next time she visited, I wanted her to start with the bed. I could awkwardly struggle in but every time was different. First she taught me how to raise and lower the bed, as well as the head, middle and foot of it. So showed me me how to get the side rails of the bed down and back up. I practiced these steps a lot. Then after I lowered one side rail and the bed, I learned how to lean over and throw one leg up on the hospital bed, holding on the rail opposite, and pull myself over far enough to pull my other leg onto the bed. Then I would turn over, reach up to the head rail, and pull myself up to the head of the bed, using my legs to push.

Again, I had no idea there were so many moves involved in a simple task like getting into bed! We practiced each time she visited. I now understood why I needed to strengthen my arms and legs! Finally I could do this successfully each time. I decided to leave the rail facing the room down and use that side exclusively. The other rail was beside a window. I needed to get into and out the bed frequently during the day and night. Getting out of bed was easy, involving resting my left hand lightly on the arm of the potty chair, placing my legs to the left and over onto the floor, then standing up or moving onto the potty.

Since I had been home, Andrew had been emptying the

potty for me each morning. I didn't think much about it. But after my therapies, I thought one morning "How embarrassing!" I decided to empty the plastic bucket myself. By holding on to my furniture and door frame with one hand, I carried the bucket carefully into the bathroom a few steps away and emptied it into the commode. I cleaned it out and brought it back to the bedside. It was maybe a little on the dangerous side but I just had to do it myself. Thank heavens I didn't drop it! Yuk!

When Dr. Perry saw this procedure she said, "Let me show you an easier and safer way to do this. Use your walker. Put the potty on the seat and then walk it into the bathroom." *Of course.*

Dr. Perry helped me walk to the bathroom and maneuver around inside, and soon signed off on that skill. I was proud. I really loved learning anything that showed me the steps to do a task safely.

Andrew had purchased a device to get into and out of the tub. Dr. Perry taught me how to use it safely. I still use it since I have not yet been able to remodel my bathroom to install a shower with wall bars instead of a tub. It consists of four legs supporting a platform. Two legs are inside and two outside the tub. She demonstrated how to sit down on the side of the platform extending out over the edge of the tub. She showed me a handle on the left inward side of the platform to grasp as I sat down. Then I was to slide to the left, pulling my legs one at a time over the lip of and into the tub. After practicing this together a couple of times, she said I had it. She then asked me to demonstrate how I would bathe.

There was a shower head high on the wall above the tub. Andrew purchased a handheld shower head which was installed low on the wall within reach, as are the water controls. I sit to shower. I have a rubber bathmat and a small non-slip rug to stand on when getting out of the tub. My towel is beside the tub, and I can dry off even before getting out. There is a bar attached to the right side of the tub and I can lean on to that bar and the tub seat while stepping over the side to the bath mat.

For safety's sake, she recommended I bring my panic button into the bathroom where it will be accessible, if I should fall. Dr. Jones thought I would be safe showering after we practiced getting in and out of the tub several times.

All of these helpful skills took two weeks to practice and master. With all of my tasks completed by late September, Dr. Jones signed off and discharged me.

I had completed all my therapy goals in a little over a month. Wow!

With my physical and occupational therapies behind me, I became interested in moving in and around the house. I was like a toddler, wanting to explore every nook and cranny. I wanted to be sure I knew where everything was so I wouldn't have to ask Andrew and Larisa so many questions.

I immediately wanted to take a shower by myself. It was a little too soon. I forgot to think through the steps first. This resulted in a setback. I got into the tub, showered and started to turn to get out of the tub. I forgot to slide to the edge and somehow ended up bending over and leaning against the back wall of the shower. My weight pushing my feet against the wet rubber mat caused it to start slipping toward the front of the shower. Soon I was straight as a board leaning over the tub stool at a 45-degree angle against the back wall. (This is called the plank position in yoga. It requires a great deal of core strength. At that point I didn't have much.)

I was trapped in this position and began to panic as I rapidly tired. I called out for Andrew and Larisa, who fortunately were at home upstairs. They came running downstairs and raced into the bathroom. They both had to work together to get me out, because by this time I was paralyzed with fear and fatigue, unable to move myself in any direction. Yet another image for Andrew to clear from his mind.

A few days later, they began to tease me about it. We still talk about my first "plank." Laughing about it helped. For a while after that I took showers only when Larisa and Andrew were both around, and I informed them when I was about to do so. However, I never made that mistake again!

We purchased a Nautilus recumbent bike to put in my bedroom for exercising. I watch television so it's not quite so boring. Of course, this has afforded me great progress in leg strength and mobility.

Chapter Twenty-One: An Undercurrent of Rumblings

When I first returned home from the nursing and rehab center, Andrew and Larisa became engaged to be married. We were all excited about the news. The wedding would take place the next summer.

Andrew had already moved back into our home permanently. At first Larisa continued to live in the house they were renting to finish packing her clothing and cleaning up the apartment. She came over almost every evening and ate dinner with us. I think it might have been her way of adjusting to living with me and was probably a good idea.

There is an ancient Chinese ideogram for "Trouble. Two females under one roof." It proved to be true. In our case I still had cognitive and physical limitations that none of us realized or understood. And I remained burdened with an Alzheimer's diagnosis. We were living in three different universes once Larisa moved in permanently at the end of September. With my physical progress I thought I was back to my old self and had no problems. But I did. I was involved in therapies, studies, new tasks, constant testing, and always challenging myself to improve. I was under stress, and so were they. Andrew had decided that working as a chef meant being away from home at night and decided to accept an offer with a friend's company specializing in large landscaping jobs. It paid significantly more money than chef work. He was still settling into his new job. Larisa was looking for one. Larisa didn't know me well and had little understanding of the many facets of Alzheimer's. None of us did.

In retrospect, I take all the responsibility for our difficulties. I had started to become angry at my limitations, my future, and Jude. I tended to take it out on Andrew and Larisa. I didn't realize this at the time.

I've consulted Andrew about this time starting in mid-October 2018, and he's told me I was extremely difficult to get along with. I've learned that Alzheimer's patients often lose their filters. Have a thought, and it comes tumbling out of your mouth. I couldn't get used to their lifestyle and food preferences. I didn't want to complain since Andrew had literally saved my life, and it seemed ill-mannered. They were doing all the cooking and cleaning. I was only washing my own clothes. I kept forgetting how Andrew and Larisa had given up their home and jobs in Oregon and driven across the country to care for me. I'm human, but now I wonder how could I have acted so badly? I was feeling guilty and shameful most of the time. With good reason.

I began cleaning up the kitchen after dinner. That way it would be clean when I came in after they left in the morning. Chefs are notorious for leaving the kitchen in a mess, using every pot, pan, spoon, and spatula and then leaving it all soiled on the counter. It annoyed me but in the scope of things it was inconsequential. I gritted my teeth and learned to make cleaning up a kind of meditative experience. Since they cooked, it was only fair that I should clean up anyway. What was I thinking? I'm not proud of myself for most of my actions during this time.

I, with too much time on my hands, began to feel unfairly critical of Larisa. I mistakenly believed Andrew had to do all the work around the house. I said so to Andrew. To his credit, he defended Larisa. However, not to my credit, this made me mad. I told him so. He became angry with me and refused to discuss it with me. Though this did not happen often, it left a bad taste in our mouths. Again I felt guilty. I just couldn't stay out of their business. I felt a loss of control over what was going on around me.

I also was jealous that Andrew gave more attention to Larisa than to me. And I was really becoming an angry person as I thought of how Jude had treated me. I know I was feeling like a child with a child's emotions every time I got upset. No one gave me or anyone permission to be upset. We had no vocabulary to vent our feelings without getting emotional.

Andrew and I had been having appointments with the psychiatrist he had originally contacted regarding my medications, Dr. Giselle Kohl. In mid-October he made an appointment to talk to her about the fact that he thought I was angry and moody. More so than usual.

Andrew told Dr. Kohl about my mood swings, angry episodes and criticisms. He said I seemed anxious all the time. I couldn't comment because I didn't fully realize how my behavior was coming across to others. Was this behavior normal for Alzheimer's patients? For example, I was sitting in my wheelchair at that moment anxiously twiddling my thumbs, a nervous habit I had at the time. I self-consciously saw Dr. Kohl looking at them. Then Giselle asked him to continue to accompany me to future visits because he seemed to have a better memory of what was happening at home. Andrew would tell her about an incident. She would ask me, "How do you feel about it?"

"He's probably right," I would say. "I don't remember it exactly like that, but I don't think he would lie."

Giselle told us that, coincidentally, she lived with her father and three sons. He had moved in with them two years previously due to the death of his wife, her mother. She said it had been extremely hard for them all to adjust. They still were working on it. She told us difficulties with a parent in the house were normal.

She stated, though, that her father, not handicapped, had helped out the family by being at home with the children when she worked. She worked long hours, having a hospital patient load as well as her private practice. Her father cooked for everyone and chauffeured the children during the day. These were positives we didn't have. She was now extremely grateful to have him in her home, she said.

I resolved inwardly to find new ways to be helpful and make them grateful, if possible. Doing the dishes were a good step. Cooking some meals was another. I had been listening.

Dr. Kohl changed my medications to keep me calmer.

However, she didn't address my Alzheimer's diagnosis. She did say I seemed anxious to her. And she was worried about my sleep problems. She hoped medications would help because I often felt out of control. I had ruminative thinking, especially in bed at night, where I would go over and over things and try to change the results of the past.

She recommended that we schedule a visit with one of her office partners, a counselor named Annie Lowe. She was excellent at helping people improve communication skills, and Giselle thought we could benefit from seeing her a few times.

We made an appointment to see her, and would continue our monthly appointments with Giselle as well. Giselle began working to decrease my anxiety and see that I got a full night's sleep. She said sleep is a way of getting rid of toxins in the brain and is very important to healing. She explained to us that a brain needs time to heal from trauma. I remembered that I had read the same thing recently. I had been reading about Alzheimer's and brain injuries.

Chapter Twenty-Two: Tincture of Time

Annie, the counselor, greeted us with a warm smile that made her office feel happy. In my mind I see her office glowing yellow. I immediately felt safe in her presence. Andrew was reserved and actually was not in favor of his participation.

It's not surprising that he was angry. After all he had done for me, why was I complaining and unhappy again? And with him. We couldn't be together long without having "words." He felt this was my problem.

Annie was direct and to the point. She asked us what we wanted to accomplish. I said, "Communicate better with Andrew." He said, "Get rid of the tension in the house."

Annie said she would give us some scripts to practice when we talked. These were written down, and she gave them to us. We were asked to practice in her office. We didn't do well. She made notes. She asked us to try again, while she suggested better words. She asked us to do our best to use the scripts when conversing. "No one can be perfect at this. You can get better. I can tell you love each other very much."

Essentially, she was telling us what I had learned during my counseling education.

Listen to the other person. Check with your partner to be sure you have understood. State what you need. Proceed in this manner. If differences arise, listen respectfully, state your own opinion and then stop talking. If things get heated, agree to disagree or shelve it until another mutually agreed upon time.

Easy to say, hard to do as emotions rise. Andrew and I tried as hard as we could to "stick to the script" during our conversations at home. We were not often successful. Andrew was also losing his patience over this laborious process. So was I. He was exactly like me!

A lot was happening to me during that fall and winter. I was having therapies, changing meds, trying to adjust to living with Andrew and Larisa, trying to learn new ways of communicating, and exercising to improve physically. I was trying to be perfect—do everything to make everything better at once and be like Andrew wanted me to be—but it was impossible and my impatience was showing.

It didn't help that seven children under the age of twelve moved in two houses down from us and fell in love with Andrew and Larisa! They were always knocking on the front door and running wild all around the outside of the house yelling at the top of their lungs if no one answered. Their divorced mother worked long hours, and they were left without supervision from morning to night seven days a week.

I became the grouchy old lady in the neighborhood who was cross with them. So they began to torture me as children do in those situations. It made me very cross indeed and drove me crazy. When I mentioned it to Andrew, he and Larisa kept saying over and over, "They're just children." They loved playing with them.

They didn't realize how much the kids were disturbing my peace and quiet.

Annie made another appointment to see me alone. She helped me to see that I was angry and there were reasons for it: my disease, my uncertain present and future, and Jude's abandonment of me when I needed him. "It's a part of grieving," she pointed out. She helped me with techniques to accept my illness, explore and dissipate the anger, including writing honestly about my feelings every night. My writing was for me alone, she said.

She asked me to make a list of positive affirmations and say them to myself before I went to sleep. She suggested I pound a pillow, take deep breathes, meditate.

She told me, "Don't deny the feelings you have. Deal with the anger you're feeling. It's perfectly natural that you would feel this way. My advice to you concerning Andrew is to give him and Larisa plenty of space. They are dealing with huge issues now. Remember not to misplace your anger onto

Andrew or Larisa. Also let him express his anger. Listen a lot. And remember you don't have to do everything at once. Give yourself time to rest and heal. Take naps every day."

I also resolved to pray and turn my troubles over to God. I prayed for God to come into my heart in this difficult time.

Though the three of us at home still had some rough moments, things slowly got better for a while as time went on. I told Andrew and Larisa I felt useless and wanted to be of more assistance to them. I told them I thought I could intellectually take on some tasks a few at a time. Andrew had taken me at my word, bless him.

First, he asked me to make phone calls to home services people we needed to schedule. Then he suggested that I look at my bank statements to familiarize myself with them and ask questions. Meanwhile I had been using the calendar given to me by Melanie, my occupational therapist from the nursing facility. She had drawn columns down each day with "To Do" on one side and "Happened Today" on the other side.

I wrote down what Andrew asked me to do and how it turned out. I also took phone messages. If a family member called to talk with me or Andrew, I wrote that down. At the end of the day, Andrew would look over the calendar. Sometimes he would write down a task for later in the week.

My entries began to improve as time went by. Andrew or I would write down a task, and I would carry it out pretty well. I began paying bills, and he kept an eye on them for me. He noticed that I was not making mistakes. He began to gain some confidence in me.

I was using the walker around the house and also walking without it, holding on to furniture. However, my coordination, fine motor skills, and memory were still somewhat compromised. I look at my handwriting on my calendar from that time and am amazed at how illegible and spidery some of it was at first. But I could see it was improving with time.

Chapter Twenty-Three: An Emotional Setback

My much-loved cat Squeeker was not doing well. She would sit on my lap and purr, comforting me when I first came home. She followed me everywhere around the house. Now she was not eating all of her food, and she was looking bedraggled. She seemed to have jerking fits every few minutes. Andrew called the vet, a neighbor of ours, who had treated Squeeker for eighteen years. He came right over.

He essentially told us that "The Squeek," one of her nicknames, was 100 years old in cat years. She had neurological problems. She was going to die soon. He examined her and told me to make her comfortable and happy for her last days. He knew she had had a good life. He was sorry, he said sympathetically, because he knew how much I loved the cat. She was extraordinarily appealing, a small long-haired tabby with green eyes. He said it would not be long.

In late October, I had placed her on my bed where she always slept. Suddenly she got up, walked a few steps, and fell down. She didn't seem to be breathing. I thought she had died. I cradled her in my arms and started crying. I called out frantically to Andrew, "Squeeker died." I was shattered with grief and sobbed inconsolably.

Andrew understood how I felt and he too was sad. He took her gently from my arms and placed her in a soft blanket. He called our vet at his home down the street, who came over and said she was in and out of consciousness, having seizures, and was suffering. "It would be the kindest thing to have her euthanized."

Again, I began crying hysterically. He stated he could do it the next day or there was a reputable place nearby that would do it immediately.

We talked about what to do. We decided to have her

euthanized that night. We couldn't stand to see her suffer. Andrew said he and Larisa would take her, sit by her, hold her, talk to her, and pet her while she "went to sleep." They did not think I should go. I couldn't imagine her dying. Larisa said that on the way home, Andrew burst into tears.

Andrew arranged for cremation by the facility and chose a beautiful wooden box with a hand carved top as a repository for her ashes. A small bronze plaque on the front said "Squeeker la Fluff," another of our nicknames for her. Several days later her ashes were delivered to us. I placed the box in my bedroom beside my bed with a picture of her where I can see her every day. I still tear up when I reminisce about her.

Losing my beloved cat was a setback for me. I wouldn't get out of bed and cried every time I thought about her. I felt hopeless, sad and to blame for her death. If I had been there, she would have remained healthy. I missed her every minute. Obviously, I overreacted. This probably had to do with her death reminding me of mine. I would die lonely and out of my mind, not even knowing where I was. Hopefully, Andrew would sit by me and hold my hand. Jude wouldn't be around, I remembered.

After that I wasn't the same for a while. Everything that had happened came crashing down around me. It seemed too much to be borne. I was no longer feeling positive and was angry again. I didn't care about scripts, exercise and such things. I did see Annie at this juncture, but my heart was not in it. I just cried and could barely express myself. She pointed out that Squeeker had been loved, and had lived a long happy life, longer than most cats. She was trying to console me, but it didn't help at the time.

She asked how I felt about my own death, and I just didn't want to talk about it. I wanted to say, "I don't care." She spoke of transference. Of my putting all my issues onto the cat. So what if she were right? They were my own feelings and I was entitled to them.

This was the last straw. I thought about how hard I had worked to get better to come home, and then my sweet cat died.

How unfair. What a cosmic joke. Why try so hard to get better? Ultimately, I was going to die no matter what. Andrew cared, but life would go on without me. My thoughts were dark. I would do nothing. Perhaps I should go back to the nursing home. I had a major pity party.

Then Andrew brought me a puzzle book. He said he thought I would like it, because it had crime puzzles to work out. There were forensic detective challenges. He remembered I liked to watch crime dramas on TV in the past, and that I liked solving problems. He said it looked like fun and would help me with my memory.

The book had a number of different kind of crimes to solve, using visual memory and forensic skills, and was hard but interesting. I began to thumb through it, and it was just difficult enough for me to pay attention. I immediately began working in the book, forgetting for the minute my morbid thoughts.

Once again, my son had come to the rescue. I got my mind on something outside of myself. The book did help me get more logical, and improved my memory and cognitive skills. And my emotions settled down.

By November of this eventful fall, I was able to move some of my books out of an antique bookcase in the dining room and into my room. It involved many trips back and forth using my walker seat, but I managed it. I was pleased with myself. We decided to use the old bookcase to house Andrew's many cookbooks. He let me arrange them. They were, and still are, conveniently accessed from the kitchen. He was pleased with it.

Chapter Twenty-Four: Guinea Pig for Alzheimer's

To add to my challenges that fall of 2018, in October I entered Dr. Medzul's Alzheimer's study. It was held at the rehab center attached to the University Medical and Trauma Center. Andrew drove me and picked me up each time I was tested.

After background information was obtained, I was tested physically and mentally, including repeat scans, during the following month. The first test was the fasting sugar test, where, after a twelve-hour fast including no water, I was asked to drink a large milkshake size cup of orange juice. Then an intravenous tube would be inserted for periodic blood samples.

The elderly nurse was new to the study (as she remarked to me) and was not skillful at inserting the needle into my arm. Due to dehydration from my overnight fast, my veins had shrunk. As the number of attempts increased, she and I became agitated. I kept showing her the vein my doctor's office used without having trouble. She failed a number of times, until she said she was going to have to find a new place and a deeper vein.

At this point, I was not happy, but kept it to myself. She plunged the needle and struck a vein. Also a nerve. It was painful. Since the blood was available at last for testing, she insisted she leave it in. It finally stopped hurting when I surreptitiously moved my arm a tiny bit.

She proceeded to inform me I had to lie on the stretcher for three hours with periodic testing. She would be out of the room. She told me there would be no way to contact her, but she said she would look in occasionally to draw test results. Ha! I already had an urgent need to urinate and told her so. I suffered from frequent urination anyway. She walked beside me wheeling the blood paraphernalia next to me. We made our way to a bathroom down the hall. It took forever it seemed. I knew I could never make that trip alone using my wheelchair and pushing the rolling stand holding the collection bags. The minute she left the room, I had to urinate again. I had a Depends diaper on, so I decided to relieve myself in it. And continued to do so for three hours because she never returned. There was no intermittent testing. I was embarrassed to call out for her. My Depends diaper was soaked at the end of the three hours.

When she at long last returned and asked me to stand up, I noticed a wet spot on the sheets. When I arrived at the bathroom, I saw that my slacks had a large wet stain where my soaked diaper was. I was too embarrassed to mention it to the nurse.

She came with me to the bathroom door and wheeled me to a break room, where I was given a snack and a drink (!). I sat in my wheelchair and didn't move until she returned to get me. I was sure everyone taking a break noticed my stained pants. She brought with her a hospital diaper which she said I could put on in the restroom. She said it was the only one she could find in the entire department. Good grief!

It was gigantic, made for a seven foot, 500-pound person at least. It took about thirty minutes for me to find a way to get it around my private parts and anchored enough to pull up my pants. The nurse had knocked on the door several times but never offered me any help. She had to keep coming back so she could wheel me back to her office.

I came out looking like my pants were stuffed. I could barely walk. I sat down in the wet seat of my wheelchair.

The last thing my nurse did was ask me to donate my brain for research after I died. What an inappropriate time for this question. "I can't make a decision just now," I said. "I'll think about it, talk to my family, and let you know."

At least they were going to wait for my death before taking my brain.

Immediately after my long morning with the nurse with no experience and the Gigantic Diapers, I was taken in a wheelchair to a room to take a computer-generated test of rapid discrimination between two different patterns. I was still discombobulated from my recent trials, and I couldn't understand the instructions on which keys to press and missed some of the differences. I did the best I could, feeling I could have done better had I had some time to calm down. That test took an hour.

But the technician said, "We're behind schedule, and we're going to have to move quickly through the rest of the afternoon." I had been there since nine o'clock that morning and was tired.

Next were two hours of memory tests. There were lists of words to remember and repeat, long involved stories to repeat verbatim, numbers to remember, words to define (I did well on this), thinking of words starting with certain letters (did well this time), and many tests I can't remember now. This was substantially different from the tests Dr. Medzul had administered at the end of my hospitalization and not as hard, in my opinion. As usual, I was provided with no results, even though I asked.

Thoroughly exhausted by now, I was wheeled to the radiology department where I waited and chatted with my handsome young male attendant outside the scheduling room for about an hour. When he discovered I had been a counselor, he told me about his life as a gay young professional, which was distracting and helped pass the time. He also said, "Your son is really good looking!" I protectively said his fiancée thought so too.

Finally, at my suggestion, he decided to check with the receptionist. She talked with the radiologist, who told us that he was backed up and couldn't take me today. Actually, I was relieved, called Andrew to pick me up and returned home. The first thing I did was to change into my regular Depends. Throwing away the Giant Diaper filled up my diaper pail! I immediately lay down for a well-needed rest.

Two weeks later I had the previously delayed scans done. We were told we would have to wait for Dr. Medzul to go over the results with us. He would call us to make the appointment.

Andrew, Larisa and I enjoyed a happy Halloween. The two of them decorated the porch with carved pumpkins, colorful lights and spooky figures I had collected over the years. One of them was a tombstone with the words, "Beware! Here lies chicken hawk." My brother Johnny had visited when Andrew was a toddler and took him all over the neighborhood to search for "Chicken Hawk." He told scary stories about it. Andrew had not forgotten that exciting night! Halloween decorating was a well-loved tradition with us. It was therapeutic for me because it was a lifelong activity and brought back happy memories. We told funny stories about past times. We gave out treats to the neighborhood children and, naturally, ate a lot of candy ourselves (M&M's for me).

We turned off our porch lights at 9:00 PM. Andrew and Larisa went to a costume party, with instructions for me to lock up, turn the alarm on, and call if I was afraid or needed anything. I immediately completed my Halloween tradition by viewing the "Exorcist." I then fell peacefully to sleep, immune to the horrors of the familiar movie. I was happy.

The day after Halloween, on November 1, 2018, Dr. Medzul met with Andrew and me. He discussed the test results briefly. "The cognitive and computer tests confirm you do have Alzheimer's," he stated with certainty. No mention was made of the brain scans. His said his study would continue with a session in fifteen months to repeat the tests. I said I didn't want to do the sugar fast test again. He said I would not have to do it. So I agreed to continue in the study.

Dr. Medzul stated, "I have to tell you, you won't be able to drive any longer." Dismayed, I asked why, and he said I might forget where I was and get lost. I told him I knew my hometown like the back of my hand, and I could draw him a map to anywhere he wished. He then said my reaction times were no longer fast enough to drive safely.

I couldn't argue with that.

Chapter Twenty-Five: Branching Out

In late fall I became determined to become active again. I wanted to start going out of my home to see people.

I joined the Elder Adult group at my church. They had a program called "Roses," women who would visit home-bound parishioners once a month. Skinner McGee, an old friend of mine, had volunteered to be my visitor. We reminisced about old times and caught up on each other's lives. We became fast friends again. Later we began doing many activities together. She had worked before her retirement as a social worker in a nursing home and was comfortable with my disabilities, mainly walking. Having an old friend to talk to was fun for me. I continued to build my confidence. I often forgot that I had Alzheimer's, good for my morale. Skinner said I didn't act like an Alzheimer's patient, and she had worked with them as a social worker.

I then discovered there was a monthly holy communion for the handicapped in the sanctuary, followed by lunch. Andrew took me the first time and placed my wheelchair beside the church pew. It was wheelchair-and-walker city down the aisles! In the dining hall I saw that I knew and remembered many of the people there. I had a wonderful time and Andrew picked me up as soon as it was over. Religion was food to my spirit. It was familiar and brought back happy memories. I began to remember the layout of the church and recognize some of the members. These social occasions were good for me and for all elderly people. Well-known places and familiar faces helped orient me.

My friend Skinner began picking me up from home for these monthly luncheons. We now found a wheelchair waiting at the church door. We enjoyed church and lunch. Leaving the wheelchair at the church, she returned me to my home after lunch and helped me up the steps to my house. What a beautiful friend from my youth! My heart warmed to the people around me.

Soon I wanted to try using my walker for getting around during the luncheons. Skinner said she could put my walker into her car, an SUV. We successfully managed the task of getting to the sanctuary and then to the luncheon. My walker was all I needed to get around. How exciting it was to be so mobile on my own!

Enthusiastic about venturing out, I discovered a local organization, the Shepherd's Center, which provided activities, transportation and other services for the elderly. I arranged for them to drive me to the grocery store and, later, doctor's appointments. I had to schedule these trips a week in advance, and I finally learned how to manage this using my calendar. I used a wheelchair provided in the grocery store and would be picked up by my driver. I would climb the stairs to my house using my railings, and the driver would carry my groceries up to my front door. The driver would assist me into the doctor's office.

Getting out of the house, independently making the arrangements, and interacting with friends and strangers made me proud. I needed it, because things were not always good at home. I still would get irritable at times. We were sometimes getting on each other's last nerve. I decided to figure out new ways to be active and stay out of their hair. I also learned not to relate every detail of my life to Andrew and Larisa. They were the only people I talked to every day, and in my enthusiasm, I wanted to share my activities and progress. They told me it was "too much information." I understood. Of course, I was not the entire focus of their lives.

I found out the public library offered a weekly classic film series. My friend Skinner and I began going to lunch at a nearby Greek restaurant we both loved, then to the library. We would watch the movie, then check out books. We had wonderful times. And I had new books to read. I could concentrate again and stay with the narrative throughout an entire novel! I was fortunate to have this escape hatch.

Normality was returning to my life in many ways.

Next a 79-year-old man (in amazing health) volunteered to drive me the block to my church to relieve Skinner of this duty. He lived alone and was awkward socially. I had become outgoing and cheerful. We chatted together amicably.

We helped each other. I helped him remember where his car keys were and reminded him to retrieve his hat from the church (!). He would steady me as we walked together into the church and to the lunch hall. This whole trip was made without my walker! Another step forward, pardon the pun. I loved being helpful in return for his help.

Chapter Twenty-Six: Landscaping During Thanksgiving

There was a great deal of confusion around the house from Thanksgiving through June of the next year. It affected me negatively. Andrew decided to make major home repairs including landscaping. It caused a lot of stress. My mood went up and down and so did Andrew's. We had bad days and good days. My anxiety levels increased again. I just seemed unable to keep in mind how helpful it was for them to get this much work done for me. Andrew and Larisa were exhausted and irritable at times. And my house was topsy-turvy again.

It was difficult for me to manage even the things for which I had been responsible. I took on too much because after all they were working on my house. There were muddy footprints in the kitchen which I had to clean up daily, just to keep my stress level down. Dirty work clothes and tools were everywhere. There was noise around me every afternoon and night. The seven young neighborhood children were enlisted to help and they were constantly hollering at each other. People were in and out of the house, getting drinks and using the bathroom. I regressed and often had to go to my room in the afternoon and evening. Stress, stress, stress! Not good for me, but how could I explain or complain?

Thanksgiving 2018 was a memorable day for me, but I later discovered it was stressful for Andrew and Larisa.

Andrew wanted to have our traditional Thanksgiving dinner for my extended family that year. He thought it would help me. He said, "Don't worry. Larisa and I will do everything." I believed it would be too much for them, since they were working day and night. He said he wanted to do it and they could handle it. As usual, my dear son was selfless and could somehow handle multi-tasking and a heavy workload. He said he and Larisa would spend the day before

111

Thanksgiving with her family.

I suggested that my family could bring some of the food. He agreed. I was delighted and invited my family. All accepted. As the day drew nearer, I began to be anxious. It seemed that their work on my house would not be finished on time, or they would not be at a stopping place by Thanksgiving Day. I worried they would not be able to plan, organize and carry off such a large family occasion, especially since they would be away the night before. I had always handled this meal, and it was a lot more work than he realized, I thought. Andrew told me later that my anxiety nearly drove him and Larisa crazy. I hadn't realized my feelings had been so obvious.

My family (my three brothers, sister and their spouses) arrived, and most of us started singing by the piano while David played, as we usually did when together. We had sung at talent shows and parties through the years. This made me remember happy occasions, and the words and my parts of the familiar songs came to me easily. Andrew and Larisa slaved away, accepting no help, setting the table and cooking special gourmet dishes to add to those brought by the family.

Andrew made a three-tier charcuterie appetizer. It was a showstopper. My brother David took pictures. He shows them to his friends even today. I had known Andrew was a skilled chef, but not that he could accomplish such a beautiful professional dish. David's wife Leigh sweetly helped out in the kitchen by giving him items as he needed them. I was impressed and proud of him. We ate far too much and talked for hours. Afterwards, my family cleaned up under Andrew's direction. I just sat in the living room and enjoyed having all of us together. Then everyone joined me there to swap family stories and sing some more. Andrew and Larisa were quiet and went up to bed early with our heartfelt thanks for the great meal. They were exhausted with good reason and maybe bored with all the family stories which we tell over and over. I still don't know how they did it all.

I can never thank Andrew adequately for thinking to give me this present in the midst of his busy life. It brought back wonderful memories of Thanksgivings past. I will never forget it. I could tell by subtle comments made by my family, however, that they thought this might be our last gathering, because I might be demented by next year. I didn't think so. To the contrary, I felt better each day. However, I did enjoy being petted and made over by them, I have to admit. I didn't protest. They meant well and were showing their love. My family is the most important thing in my life, I have discovered. More so since my diagnosis. I was forgetting that diagnosis more and more often. It was good that I didn't dwell on it but remained positive in my thinking. I've read that positive thinking goes a long way in recovery from illness.

Chapter Twenty-Seven: Christmas and Landscaping

Soon it was Christmas 2018. Andrew and Larisa drove to the mountains to get and cut down a tree, a family tradition, and we all decorated it with my fifty-year old collection of ornaments. Each one brought back a memory to me. I loved it. They made the front porch beautifully festive with the lights we always used over the years.

I made all my presents, including a botched knitted scarf for Larisa which I turned into a hot pad in her favorite color. It turned out knitting was too much for me to handle! I also painted pictures for them and ordered a few other items. I wrapped them and arranged them under the tree. I placed candy in the stockings hanging from the mantel. There would be a walnut and tangerine in the toe as usual. There were also intriguing looking presents under the tree for me. The living room looked festive and merry and my spirits were high.

Andrew and Larisa spent Christmas Eve with her parents and other relatives and then returned late that night. Christmas Day, we celebrated together at our home. We opened presents, taking turns, including pink flannel pajamas for me. Looking at myself in the mirror, I saw that they lit up my face. I couldn't stop smiling.

Suddenly Andrew asked me to go to my bedroom for a moment. He then came to get me and said, "Close your eyes, Mom."

He walked me into the living room and told me to open my eyes. There sitting in a chair beside the tree was the largest stuffed teddy bear I had ever seen, bigger than I was! They gave me a written letter "from Santa." They asked me to read it aloud to them, since they hadn't read it, wink, wink. I reproduce it here.

"Dearest Dianne,

worry. They're locked up and can't get out. The outside door around the corner from your room is always kept locked. Anyway, I'll be sure you're safe."

What did she mean 'be sure I'm safe'? Was she unsure the men would be locked up each night? Would the door around the corner from me be locked 100 per cent of the time? Of course not, I knew. Thank heavens the medicine she administered put me to sleep quickly, ending my torment and fear.

Later on during my stay, when I was able to be up and around in my room, I looked out of my window and saw a large institutional-type building on a short hill above our facility. There was a tall chain-link fence between it and my building. Upon investigation, I saw there was a heavy door to the outside around the corner from my room. I felt safer.

I heard the howling several times a week during my six-week-long stay in the facility. It never frightened me again, though it made me have the uncanny feeling that I was in a horror movie. But I began to see some humor in my situation.

Those poor howling men were my first zombies.

Another night soon after that, I heard a woman shrieking in an ascending tone, "Char-lee, Char-lee? Where are you? I know you're there. Stop teasing me. Come on to bed."

She cried out over and over and over. I felt anxious for her. Where were the nurses? Where was Charlie? Why wasn't he answering her? Finally I heard two nurses stomp down to her room across the hall from me. They were clearly mad and said a few mean things to and about her. I could hear them. She became quiet a short while after they entered her room. They exited the room still complaining about her.

I quizzed the morning meds lady, who had become my news source, about the incident. She said blithely, "That's Yvonne, the woman across the hall from you, calling out to her husband. He's dead. She thinks he's alive. She's lost her mind."

This was so blunt and cruel a speech, I was shocked beyond words. The nurse said, "She does this almost every night, so turn your TV volume up loud, and you won't hear her."

I've known that you have had a difficult year, and I wanted to give you something extra special this Christmas, because I've watched how hard you have been working. So, I had my elves make this great big bear just for you! I had them make it extra big and soft, in case you ever feel like you need a hug. We also made a deal with Andrew and Larisa to get you a year's subscription to The New Yorker magazine, because they told me you've been missing it. I hope you know that I love you, and be sure to give your new bear lots of snuggle time while you read in the new year.

Sincerely yours,
Santa"

I burst into tears. I could barely speak to say how grateful I was for their thoughtfulness. Teddy now lives in my bedroom. He sleeps with me from time to time though he hogs the bed. What a sweet gift!

Andrew also gave me a tiny pewter wizard which looked exactly like my friend the blue wizard (remember him?), except he's carrying a Christmas tree. I can't figure out how he knew exactly what he looked like. Andrew is close-mouthed on the subject. It sits on the bookcase bedside my bed so I can see him every day.

Christmas was wonderful for me. More than I can express. I felt even better.

Chapter Twenty-Eight: A New Year and Giant Steps

January 2019 was the start of new activities. I had begun socializing, handling some simple home tasks, and becoming enthusiastic about my future. I didn't think about my Alzheimer's. It didn't occur to me to worry about getting worse. I was too busy.

Andrew and Larisa were working during the day and most nights. They decided to rescue a rambunctious black lab puppy, Reese, and she moved in with us. She introduced a whole new level of confusion to our family. I wondered if I could stand it, especially as I was responsible for her during the day. Why did they keep adding new situations to our lives? I think they didn't understand my stress level since I was getting so much better. Luckily, I liked dogs. She would bark when someone came to the door and jump all over the person who entered. Finally, Andrew and Larisa installed a crate to contain him when visitors came into the house. They took him for frequent runs in the park down the hill from our home to help dissipate some of his energy.

I felt safe by myself during the day with the dog. Also, Andrew installed a home security system. Unfortunately I wasn't able to walk Reese because he liked to chase squirrels and could pull me down. Eventually he would come when I called him, so I could let him out for short trips to the backyard during the day, a big help to Andrew and Larisa.

On January 19, 2019, we all celebrated my seventy-fifth birthday. Each of my brothers and sisters called to sing happy birthday to me, a tradition in our family. Andrew and Larisa made a cake decorated with a multitude (!) of candles we blew out together. There were balloons and flowers on the table. They gave me a birthday hat that reminded me of a wizard. They teased me about my "three quarters of a century." We talked about old times when Andrew was young. Larisa talked about her experiences as a child. I enjoyed the evening and was genuinely happy. I felt like an important member of the family. All this was making me happy and hopeful for the future.

I had several routine physician visits throughout the winter and spring and was able to arrange my own transportation. My visits to the church, the library and lunch with my longtime friend Skinner kept me busy. I was riding my recumbent bike, practicing yoga, reading, and working in my crime puzzle book. I played Mah Jongg and Solitaire on the computer. I watched re-runs of Jeopardy, challenging my brain to answer questions before the contestants. I often could! I was paying bills and I also planning and cooking meals more frequently. I knew at last that I could help the family. I was a useful person!

My cognitive powers seemed to be returning every day in spite of the confusion around the house. I began to think about abstract things such as my life and what it had meant, my diagnosis, and my personal philosophy. I enjoyed time alone as well as with friends. I could see I was making slow progress toward living a rich life again. All of the activities I had decided to take on were reaping benefits to my cognitive health.

I thought of my family members often. I became outwardly grateful and thankful. I went over my blessings before bed and first thing in the morning. I developed a routine and made lists so I wouldn't forget to turn off the stove (I had done it once), turn the alarms on and off (had forgotten to do this a few times), take my pills (had forgotten twice), and other things I might forget if I got distracted. I learned to cope with the fact that I could concentrate on only one thing at a time. These things helped my feeling of security at managing my home.

My schedule of future activities was accurate and I could make plans for the future.

Chapter Twenty-Nine: An Important Email and a Wedding

After trying and failing to reach Dr. Medzul by phone, in April 2019 I decided to send him an email telling him of my improvements. I more and more fervently believed I didn't have Alzheimer's and desperately wanted to discuss this with him. I was certain that a mistake had been made. I was not getting worse over time. Every day I was talking to people who would say, "You don't act like you have Alzheimer's."

My email read, edited for clarity:

"Dear Dr. Medzul:

I have finished all my Phase I testing in your study and your neurologists gave me a diagnosis of "dementia."(Alzheimer's) I don't like this term. I'm writing you to tell you I've begun to walk without assistance, am engaging in social activities, making new friendships, taking courses and attending lectures. I'm using my computer again. My new friends and my family tell me they think I've been misdiagnosed. Is this possible? During my cognitive testing as a part of Phase I of your study, I was upset and fatigued the day of the testing. I believe I'm better than the tests indicated. And I'm a lot better than the day you tested me prior to that. I would appreciate your taking another look at the scans I was given in your study and see what you think."

Sincerely,
Dianne Hobbs

I received no immediate reply. I resolved to be patient. He was a busy man and would have to take the time to obtain and read the test results. On the other hand, he must know how important this was to me. Months went by and I still didn't hear from Dr. Medzul. I had expected to hear from him long before now. I wondered about whether I should phone his office or email him again. But then activity at home got really, really busy. It slipped my mind

Landscaping work was completed in the back and front yards. Andrew did all the stonework of building walls and a huge brick patio with benches and lights. It turns out he has many talents as a stonemason. Andrew and Larisa wanted to plan and make all the arrangements for their wedding to be held in June. They wanted it to be held in our backyard. Oh my lord. No wonder they had worked so hard to make it beautiful! My good luck! I was actually delighted that it would take place at our home, though I worried that I would become anxious during the comings and goings. But I offered to help in any way they wanted.

Wedding and bridesmaids' dresses were chosen, groomsmen outfitted in tuxes, and I bought a new dress which I thought was beautiful and made me feel special. I hadn't dressed up since before my fall. Larisa's brother, a minister was going to officiate. The backyard was beautifully decorated with a tent and flowers. I was thrilled that my son was so happy to be getting married.

In the blink of an eye, it was June 21, 2019, their wedding day. The work had been completed on time. What an experience it had been for us all, both bad and good. We had made it through with our love intact, no small feat!

My job for the wedding was to help Andrew make and ice the almond mandarin orange wedding cake (his own recipe). It felt good to know he trusted me with this task. Andrew's father had traveled from California for the wedding. Together at the kitchen table he and I ground the almonds for the flour and made the icing. Our first cooperative effort ever, and actually quite fun. I had worried about being with my ex-husband but many years had passed since I had seen him. It was no effort at all to be friends. I was proud of my new attitude.

All around the house, the wedding party was arriving and dressing in various rooms. The atmosphere was filled with talking and laughter. Andrew even survived when one of his friends, also a chef, accidentally threw half the cake icing into the garbage can. Andrew calmly made another batch. All the bustle and confusion didn't bother me at all this time. It was fun. Mirabele dictu! (My mother's favorite expression: "Wonderful to relate." She loved throwing Latin expressions into everyday conversations.)

The wedding was beautiful and moving. The traditional bride and groom dance was followed by the parents' dances with their children. Andrew and I had been practicing the shag, a southern swing dance, on our patio so I would have confidence that I wouldn't fall. He actually swung me in a pirouette to the applause of all the guests. This by a lady who was in a wheelchair the previous year! How proud and delighted we were. I didn't use my walker once!

It had been a sweet, joyful and romantic wedding. The next morning, Andrew and Larisa left for a month-long honeymoon in Kathmandu, Nepal. We openly told each other this would a good break from each other!

After seeing them working together over the previous months, I knew their marriage was on solid ground. I had no doubts at all as to their future. I was calm in my mind about them. I was proud of them. A calm mind was just what I needed after all the frantic house, work and wedding prep of the preceding months. All in all it helped me to feel proud of my progress and very happy about the future. I felt pretty normal.

Chapter Thirty: Family Gathering at the Beach

I couldn't stay alone for a month, so my family (except for brother Jim who declined) planned a house party at the beach. This turned out to be a turning point in my family's attitude toward me. My brother David drove me there, and we all had an unforgettable holiday. The weather was perfect, and the long walks to and from the beach were therapeutic for me. I didn't carry my walker with me to the beach and got along fine without it. I felt really strong and more capable than I knew. My family was frankly surprised and delighted by my progress. They called me a rock star!

Having always loved shelling on the beach and swimming, I did both. The surf was rough one day and David had to help me out past the shore but riding up and over the waves had come back easily to me. I actually rode waves in to the shore on a small rubber raft. I hadn't forgotten how to do that! Walking through the surf back out to the waves had not been easy though. Waves would knock me to my knees, over and over. I laughed so hard I couldn't walk in the shifting water. Finally, David came and helped get me upright. People on the beach were smiling and laughing with us as we came out of the water. I loved it. No one there thought I had Alzheimer's! My brother David was also responsible for a big step forward in my independence. I had a medicine regime that involved pill boxes. I took different medicines morning, noon and night, and they differed from day to day. Andrew had written extensive instructions for David who soon figured out a much simpler system. I immediately caught on and from then on was able to manage my own meds. Another breakthrough for me!

Chapter Thirty-One: Beginning A New Beginning

After the beach trip, my family returned to their homes. I stayed with David and his wife Leigh at their home in New Bern, North Carolina. They had a large group of friends in their boating community but a small house. I soon discovered that I wasn't comfortable being with a noisy crowd of total strangers. I became jittery and uncomfortable. Finally, I told David that I had to go home. I had learned to ask for what I needed. He drove me home the next day and stayed with me overnight to be sure I was settled in. He made no complaints. He is and has always been a dear brother. I had called a neighbor who said she would look in on me daily until Andrew and Larisa returned. Instead, my sister Elizabeth sweetly volunteered to drive the fourteen hours from her home in Alabama to stay with me a few days of that last week before the honeymooners returned.

She had helpfully been pursuing extensive research on Alzheimer's disease and shared a lot of her findings with me during her stay. This information became extremely helpful to me. She gave me the address of an on-line Alzheimer's forum which I joined and learned new facts about my disease and its inevitable progress. I realized that I really was not going downhill as was expected. My sister also told me she was doubtful about my diagnosis. I now was sure I really didn't have the disease. There had been a mistake. I was sure that Dr. Medzul would eventually confirm it. My sweet generous sister stayed with me three days before returning home. I frankly enjoyed the peace and quiet before Andrew and Larisa returned. The next three days alone was a tremendous relief. I discovered I could manage well on my own. I enjoyed the peace and quiet. I relaxed and became calm. I took naps and slept well at night. I cooked for myself. I took my pills.

My family's support provided encouragement, support and
assistance with skills I needed to be able to take care of myself.
I am grateful to them beyond words.

Andrew and Larisa returned from their honeymoon in late
July of 2019.

During the fall of 2019, both Andrew and Carolina were
working full time. She held two half-time counseling positions.
Andrew was continuing his work for a landscaping firm. He
discovered he loved landscaping. He and his friend were
growing a booming business.

Andrew arranged to have a new kitchen floor installed. It
now had cushioned tiles and was a significant improvement to
the previous linoleum floor. It had made walking around the
kitchen more comfortable for me, since I was now walking
barefoot around the house. I had started this practice at the
beach and had found it made me feel more stable. I could sense
my feet on the sand and floor.

During the early fall, I maintained my progress. My former
activities had increased now that I was alone each day.
Following up on my sister's information, I had discovered a
transportation service for people who couldn't drive. Small
green buses would transport us all over the town from 6:00 AM
to 10:00 PM daily. I would call the morning before my planned
trip, the operator would ask me where I wanted to go, what time
I had to be there and what time I wanted to be picked up to
return home. She would give me a fifteen-minute window to
either side of the target arrival time, when the bus would pick
me up. I could cancel up to the morning of the rides. This was
absolute and total freedom for me. No one person had to drive
me around. I began to look independently for local activities I
had enjoyed in the past or new ones available to me.

I contacted the Shepherd's Center which had previously
provided transportation for me. I learned they offered a
plethora of activities for elderly persons, on and off site. I
requested a copy of their schedule and learned they paid for art
classes at a prestigious art school nearby. I immediately signed
up for a five-week watercolor class. I had previously studied

and worked in oil, pen and ink, and pencil and liked the look of watercolors. Learning new things was good for brain, my sister and my son had told me. On my own, I scheduled a bus to take me to my first class in September 2019. It arrived promptly on time and dropped me off five minutes early. I was picked up ten minutes after the class ended. This system was going to work! The participants were delightful and we chatted among ourselves happily. The attractive, middle-aged teacher, Leslie Karpinski, was a dynamic, inspiring and talented local artist. The ladies in the class had various levels of experience, enabling us to learn from each other. Art came back into my life!

All of us loved the class so much that we requested a follow-up class with Leslie. It was held during the next month, October 2019. I began doing watercolors at home. I gave some of my pictures to family members for Christmas that year and hung others in my home.

During October I began taking water-walking classes at the local YMCA, two days a week. This strengthened my legs so much that I began walking the two blocks to the Y and back home without a walker. My happiness knew no bounds. It seemed the more I did, the more I wanted to do.

I scheduled activities frequently during the week. I became a regular on the bus. I must say with a laugh that many of the roads on my routes had not been well-maintained, and the buses were old with weak shocks. The seat belts were loose and were not effective in keeping me from bouncing all over the place. With both hands, I would hold onto any seat or window ledge I could reach. If you sat over the wheels, it was a particularly rough ride. The passengers sat one to a seat. The front seat was the best ride. The first arrival would always take that seat. Wheelchair patients were strapped down tightly to the floor and, lucky for them, did not move. I usually ended up over a wheel.

Sometimes, an especially rough bump would jolt all of us up off our seats. You could see all the heads rise and sink back down in unison. One day, the driver had gone too fast around a curve and over a pothole. I bounced up about six inches, and my purse popped out of the seat. The contents spilled out all over the floor. Everything went everywhere, including under the seats. The bus driver had to stop the bus, and we all gathered up my things. What a sight that must have been! I smiled about it every time I thought about it for weeks afterward. I learned I could accommodate to different situations, even surprising bus bumps.

On another memorable occasion, a bus pickup had necessitated going up a street where there was road construction. Either side of the road had wide cavernous holes with men working down inside. There was barely enough room for the bus to pass through. We had to negotiate this twice, up and back. We all peered fearfully out the windows down into the craters, imagining the bus toppling over. We all loudly applauded the driver when we passed the ditch.

She laughed and said, "That was a tight one all right! I'm glad I made it."

I hadn't known there was any doubt about it!

In November 2019 I took another art course called "Cut Paper Art." The instructor provided pre-cut cardboard shapes, glue and card stock in different colors. She demonstrated some methods and ideas, and then we were on our own. We were invited to walk around and see other's techniques and ideas. I made Christmas and All Occasion cards. Our homemade cards looked surprisingly like store-bought ones. Another new skill learned!

My brain has regained its creative bent. Arts and crafts enrich my life tremendously.

Chapter Thirty-Two: I Don't Have Alzheimer's!

On October 28, 2019, five long months after my email to my doctor, a miracle occurred. I was called from Dr. Medzul's office and told over the phone by his assistant: *"**You don't have Alzheimer's Disease! Dr. Medzul looked over your scans and says he no longer believes you were given the correct diagnosis. He wants you to make an appointment to go over the scans with him.**"*

Ecstatic, I shouted loudly, "What did you say? Are you sure?" She repeated the news. "Dr. Medzul will discuss it with you." Andrew had heard me and rushed to my room. And she told him what she told me. I began crying and laughing at the same time. I remember saying, "Thank God!" I couldn't stop my exultation. Andrew and I were jubilant.

At the same time, we could not fully believe it. We were stunned. How could such a thing have happened? Why had I had to question the diagnosis before it was changed? Why had it taken five months for Dr. Medzul to reply to my email? I was in his study and he said he would be closely involved with me. Why had the mistake not been discovered sooner? Why had my family and I had to suffer through *over two years* of anxiety, fright about the future, and negative expectations? Why had we been forced to imagine me without my mind, drooling, recognizing no family members, requiring around-the-clock nursing care, essentially a vegetable? This was unforgivable. Both of us were confused and upset with Dr. Medzul.

But we were so happy, these thoughts was not at the forefront of our minds. We just kept smiling at each other every time we saw one another. I called everyone in my family and gave them the news. All were, of course, thrilled and, at the same time, puzzled as to what had happened. I said I would let them know after my meeting with Dr. Medzul. This was scheduled for January 2020, **three months after the phone call.** He is a busy man, indeed! I was resentful at the delay. After all it was his mistake and had caused undue suffering. I was not so important to him or his study after all.

I regrouped enough to call his secretary back, saying I would like to be given driving privileges immediately. One more call arrived from Dr. Medzul's office scheduling me with an occupational therapist for a driving test. I passed with flying colors on November 19, 2019, a red-letter day for me. I guess my reaction time was not now a problem. *Free at last!* The remainder of 2019 was occupied with driving to art classes, shopping at farmer's markets, visiting friends, reading, painting and taking care of my chores in the house. I loved being able to drive and got more confident as time wore on.

I spent this Thanksgiving with David and his wife Leigh, along with my youngest brother Johnny and his wife Diane. (David picked me up and drove there and back. He thought it was too long a drive for me to make alone. I'm so very grateful to him.) We all brought dishes to share. David, Leigh and I made traditional Thanksgiving food. Diane brought a delicious Greek dish as we always ask her to do. As usual in my family, we stuffed ourselves and laughed a lot. We find each other totally amusing. In the late afternoon after dinner, we took a long cruise on the Neuse River on David and Leigh's Hatteras boat. It was a warm sunny day and absolutely beautiful on the water. We cruised along the shore, peacefully viewing the shoreline. We gazed quietly and happily at the sunset as we returned to the neighborhood dock. Quite a memorable day for relaxing and chatting happily with my two brothers and their wives. Boating with my family brought back happy memories of boating during family vacations at our lake cottage at High Rock Lake near Piedmont.

The next day David and I decorated his Christmas tree while Leigh visited her daughter's family for a few days. She is no longer into decorating large trees after the twelve-foot one foisted upon her the Christmas before. It took three men to get it into their house and took up the entire dining room. David always says, "Hey, the bigger the better." He had a thousand lights on that tree, he claims without disagreement from his wife. We had fun unpacking his ornaments, many with a nautical theme. There were lighthouses, boats, lobster traps, starfish, sand dollars, Santas and reindeer surfing, and so many more that Leigh eventually laid down the law: no more nautical decorations! David likes collecting ornaments as much as I do. No two ornaments of the same color could be beside each other, was his rule. Of course, he had his own ideas of how to put on the Christmas lights. He had hundreds of lights and ornaments. I must say it turned out like a magazine picture. I took pictures of it to remember always. We lit a fire, had hot chocolate, and sang together while he played Christmas carols on his keyboard. These familiar activities brought to mind a lifetime of happy memories.

Chapter Thirty-Three: Independent Living

In December after Christmas, Andrew, Larisa and I began discussing alternate living arrangements. We had touched on this topic before. Andrew was now confident I could live alone, and so was I. Andrew and Larisa needed their own space and privacy. It seemed to me the best thing to do was for them to stay in my large house. I would move to a small apartment. I said I would look for one. At the time, they were in agreement. I drove all over town looking at apartments and then asked a neighbor about the house she was living in. There was a vacant apartment beside her. I had found an apartment right across the street from my house! It was a large apartment and affordable. Andrew, Larisa and I talked about the apartment. I could sense their reluctance. I suddenly realized they needed more distance from me to feel independent. What had I been thinking!

They suggested that we look at senior resident facilities with graduated levels of care, beginning with independent living. These would have medical staff available on the premises for emergencies, mainly for those needing nursing or memory care but available to all. It sounded good to me. I found numerous facilities which were available and offered what we wanted. I made appointments for us to see several of them on weekends.

The first facility we visited had the welcome mat out for us. The director (of marketing we discovered) greeted us at the door with flowers and a sign with my name. Our tour of the large facility covered the art room, the living areas, the dining room (meeting the chef), and were invited to visit some selected residents in their rooms. We looked at the activities calendar. We saw studio and one-bedroom apartments. Pets were allowed. There were residents sitting in wheelchairs in the lobby area looking bored, but happy to see us.

We were led to the office and offered refreshments. Andrew said he was going to the restroom and disappeared for half an hour. Larisa and I ate all the refreshments, asked questions, looked at brochures of services offered and made as much small talk as we could. Andrew returned, asked about prices and said we would think about it. We were then offered a deal, if we would decide right then and there. I immediately thought of timeshares. I really hate that tactic. Again, Andrew said we'd consider it and let her know. We got into the car and began talking. I didn't share my feeling that I couldn't picture myself living there. The patients all seemed listless. They were not vital, active people as I considered myself to be. I asked Andrew and Larisa what they thought about it. As one they said this was not the place for me. They were both depressed. They said all the people there acted and looked older than I. I happily agreed.

Andrew had not gone to the restroom when he left us in the office. He had walked around the facility and chatted with the residents he came across. He said the much-touted cafeteria "chef" served starchy, overcooked food, and the residents had frequently complained to management about it. The residents he talked to were not happy and didn't think much of the "activities" on the calendar. You had to pay extra for any outside trips and many of the personal services.

He said he and Larisa would not want me in a facility, and they didn't want to look at any more of them. We would discuss the matter further, they said.

When we did so soon afterward, they told me they believed I would be happier staying in my own home surrounded with my own things. It would be better for me and not as stressful as changing to a new place. They said they would be happier in a small house which they could decorate to their tastes. I could see the wisdom of this. It finally hit me that Andrew truthfully didn't want to move me out of my home. I also realized that we could move me into an apartment anytime in the future that we made such a decision. By staying in my home I could still have coffee on my front porch overlooking the trees in my yard and the park down the hill. I could still hear the high school band practicing in the fall, and the football and baseball teams training. I could watch the sunset from my porch every day.

Andrew and Larisa soon found a house to rent and moved quickly. Unbelievably, they and their dog Reese moved in the first week of January 2020. I knew we had made the right decision. Then I suddenly realized how much I would miss them. But they were close enough to visit anytime and they were available if needed.

Chapter Thirty-Four: My Doctor's Prognosis for Me...and Himself

It was January of 2020 and time for my long-awaited appointment with Dr. Medzul. I went alone. He showed me my original scans and the updated ones from his study. He pointed out the areas of my brain from which the diagnosis of Alzheimer's had been made. "So I was misdiagnosed," I said. Upon his more recent look, the scan results were equivocal, he said. This meant "open to more than one interpretation." I could tell he didn't want to use the word "misdiagnosed." He also didn't bring up that he had previously had his secretary call to tell me he thought my diagnosis was incorrect. He said the cognitive testing results upon discharge from the hospital had indicated to him and his team that it was Alzheimer's, more than the scans did. My email had convinced him to take a second look. My private thoughts were that Jude's opinion, stated authoritatively to all my doctors, had carried disproportional weight with them. Also Dr. Medzul should have known not to test me, an elderly person, when I had just been admitted to the hospital. Or have me tested for his study in such a nightmarish all-day session with no respite between tests.

Dr. Medzul also said he knew I didn't have it, because "*Alzheimer's patients don't get better. You clearly are much better.*"

This was the first time I had heard him say that. I had known instinctively I was improving daily. His confirmation made my day, to say the least. I was elated. His explanation of the wrong diagnosis was troubling to me, however.

I asked him what I did have. What was my current diagnosis?

He said the scans showed some evidence my fall might have contributed to the development of hydrocephalus but he couldn't be sure. Does the reader remember what Dr. Reynolds, the first neurologist I saw, had diagnosed in March of 2018? Possible hydrocephalus! And Jude had disagreed, setting off a terrible chain of events. But there was still no certain diagnosis. Dr. Medzul repeated what Dr. Reynolds had said. "That diagnosis would account for all your past symptoms. But so could have Alzheimer's, which you don't have."

"Fortunately," he said, "you are not exhibiting any of the symptoms of hydrocephalus now. However, if you do have it, the pockets in your brain could fill up again with fluid and put pressure again on your brain. But they might not." Dr. Medzul said, "I could do a spinal tap now and remove and some fluid from your brain to make a definite diagnosis of hydrocephalus. If definite, at that time you would be put under anesthesia and surgeons would place a shunt deep into your brain so the fluid could continuously drain into your lower body. Which I don't recommend."

This invasive procedure did not sound at all like something I cared to do, ever.

"Or, we could do nothing, unless you have new symptoms."

Of course, I asked him exactly what these symptoms would be. What should I watch out for?

He said I would have some or all of the following symptoms: "Your feet will feel heavy as if stuck to the floor like concrete, you will have bowel and urinary problems and mood changes, you might lose some cognitive skills, among other milder symptoms." I got the feeling he didn't think I had to worry about this happening.

I asked him my prognosis.

He said, "The same as mine. I don't know, except we all will come to the same end. And we don't know when that will occur." Evasive, I thought.

He then asked me if I would remain in his study. I asked why. He said I was the exception to all his study participants, and he would like to follow me and include my data in his study.

I decided not to continue. I didn't want to be a guinea pig. And I didn't trust him.

I have since learned that there is no current diagnosis in my records for either Alzheimer's or hydrocephalus. So I'm an enigma! All of this testing and worry and still no diagnosis! Unbelievable.

After his move, Andrew assured me he would take care of my yard, any house repairs, or heavy lifting. He assured me he could get to my house quickly if I had an emergency. He would be notified on his cell phone if my home security system engaged and would immediately call or come over. And he has done so. Andrew began a practice of calling me or swinging by my house frequently. We both find this reassuring. I'm always happy to see him or hear from him.

I was invited to their home for dinner on my seventy-sixth birthday, January 19, 2020. They treated me like royalty. They had invited David, who drove up from New Bern and made us a homemade chocolate cake. He obsessed for hours over the swirls on the top of the cake. He really is a card. Andrew cooked a gourmet dinner and it was superb. It was a happy occasion and sealed my recovery. My brain was healed. Maybe a miracle had occurred. God surely intervened.

It disturbs me that no one has told me with certainty what happened to me. I believe my previous fall, all the psychiatric medicines I was put on, my infection and hospitalization, and subsequent move to the nursing home together caused my severe disorientation, and physical and mental decline. My cognitive tests were given too soon in less than ideal circumstances and were therefore not indicative of my actual abilities. My partner's insistence on his diagnosis of Alzheimer's undoubtedly influenced the doctors as they all discussed my scans and cognitive test results.

Chapter Thirty-Five: Life Without Alzheimer's

I realize that by living alone I can do anything I want. Or do nothing. I love the feeling! After all this time, I'm really beholden to no one. I can relax for the first time in my life. There's no one to take care of but me. It's my choice. I can watch television, take naps, read, write, or paint as I wish. As I get up each morning and look around me, I have become aware of how all life is interconnected. I also marvel at the amazing complexity of the world given to us. I realize it would take a lifetime to list all the variations of experience we've been given to enjoy. Each day I thank God for the many gifts I've been given, the latest and most miraculous of which is my gift of new life. I believe my greatest accomplishments during the last several years have been never to give up in the face of difficulties, always to remain positive in outlook, and always to trust my intuition.

I spend a lot of time pondering my experience and thinking about how lucky I am, through the intervention of a lot of people and God.

I've been blessed with a loving son, a healed brain, a close family and good friends.

Andrew is good. Life is good. God is good.

The Beginning

My Personal Observations on Patient Care

The following comments are based on my many years of hospital volunteer work, my personal experiences of treatment I received from medical professionals, and my thirteen years with my partner Jude, a neuropsychiatrist, who told me everything he knew about medical training and practices. I paid attention and remembered. I also observed him in his interactions with his peers and how he influenced my diagnosis. These are my personal opinions.

FIRST, it would help if families and visitors approach patients slowly and quietly, speak normally, and ask how they are, what treatments they're getting, and what kind of day they're having. Visitors who talk on and on about themselves force the patient to try to listen and be polite about matters that are foreign to her life at the moment. It is extraordinarily tiring and, later, depressing. It made me reflect on my lack of importance to the visitors and wonder if they saw me as having nothing to important to say.

SECOND, I believe doctors are not infallible experts. Medicine is part science, part art, and the science is not exact. The method of differential diagnosis is imprecise. However, it's the gold standard of the diagnostic process. All known symptoms are listed in medical books, categorized into families of illnesses, assigned a name, and thrown out for discussion during rounds. This is where interns are trained by residents, more experienced doctors. In rounding, doctors stand around and talk about the different diagnoses with similar symptoms but *not exactly the same.* All possible diagnoses are examined.

Or are they? There can be missed symptoms through faulty history-taking, rushed and inadequate clinical observation, previous bias, or just an unknown disease. There can be several diseases co-existing with or masking other symptoms. Illnesses can manifest differently in the elderly.

Doctors are taught to speak with certainty when diagnosing a patient, even to the extent of mentioning a different, equally likely, diagnosis. Even in that case, however, the doctor usually states his opinion. In forming it, he can be swayed by his own prejudices. A second or third opinion should sometimes be requested. Though one may hesitate to ask for this, doctors are trained not to take this personally. I should have done this but it didn't even cross my mind. I have learned my lesson the hard way.

The elderly patient can be confused by the explanation of different treatments for which each diagnosis calls. The doctor must explain what the treatment options are and is taught to use such phrases as "may make better," "uncertain outcome," or rarely, "we don't know." Hardly ever do they say, "could make worse." Just listen to the endless list of side effects listed in TV commercials touting new drugs. Has the reader noticed that many side effects are the very symptoms the medicine is supposed to treat? Or, as in my Alzheimer's and many other diagnoses, no treatment is available *at this time.*

Another issue is "prognosis," or "what will the outcome of my illness be"? Whatever the outcome may be, doctors are taught to encourage the patient. Even certain death can be couched in some vague date in the future, such as from one to six months, or "We can't be sure," and so on.

Most importantly, especially since this turned out to be true in my case, the doctors should have thought to consider the possibility something other than Alzheimer's was causing my symptoms, particularly since I was over seventy. I had been critically ill. Suddenly I was wrenched out of my home, brought to an unfamiliar place surrounded by unfamiliar faces, questioned by strangers, having different and painful procedures performed daily, and not knowing why. It makes me anxious thinking about it. It's a well-known fact that elderly people often deteriorate mentally under these circumstances. Jude's insistence on the diagnosis of Alzheimer's Disease surely influenced the doctors, even though he was retired and not on staff.

THIRD, accurate family medical histories are vital to this process of finding a diagnosis. However, hardly anyone carries this information around in their pocket. It should be close at hand in case an elderly family member becomes ill. If not, the family member must rely on his memory. This is hardly an optimum time for such reflection. In my opinion, someone with intimate knowledge of the patient should always accompany an elderly patient to the doctor or hospital. This is especially important if the person is seriously ill or compromised cognitively.

Of course, an accurate written list of all allergies and prescriptions, over the counter and herbal remedies should always be available to the person who will accompany the patient. You should always know exactly what the purpose of each medication is. This will save time and may save a life. Your pharmacist is a good source for this information as well as possible drug interactions. Just ask.

FOURTH, patients and their families should not meekly stand by without asking challenging questions. Try not to be timid about this. A family member should be available to speak for you. If an explanation is not understood, ask for it to be repeated. Have the family member take notes.

If you feel you or your loved one is not being treated courteously or professionally, ask to speak to a supervisor. If that doesn't take care of the situation, every hospital has an ombudsman trained to handle just such complaints. If a doctor's office is rude, leaves you or your relative waiting for long periods, or doesn't return calls within a day, speak to the office manager. And you can always change providers.

FIFTH, insist that you or your relative be treated as a person, not a body. It's easy to recognize the symptoms of a cold, distancing approach. And remember, the proper personal approach doesn't take much time, so don't be afraid to speak to a supervisor. A reassuring touch and a smile make a world of difference. Remember both you and your relative are distinct from all other human beings, and worthy of love, compassion and care. You should be treated as if you are a member of the medical professional's family. Insist on it. In fact, I have learned that many people ask their doctor, "What would you do if this were your mother (child, sister, wife)?" Doctor's always have to think before answering this question, and often are more frank with you.

I believe doctors should tell the patient before and after testing a brief description of what is going on and for what purpose the tests are given. I was just rolled out of my room with no explanation. Tell the patient, "We'll be taking you to X-ray now," "I'd like to take you to a group of doctors from my department who want to ask some questions. Is that all right?" And maybe give the patient an indication of the results later, even if just to say, "You did well."

If medical personnel could only know what inner life is like for confused patients, they would not talk in front of them without looking at and including them in the conversation. They would ask them questions about their thoughts and fears. They would listen attentively to the answers. They would reassure the patient. They would smile and look into the patient's eyes. They would touch the patient as they talked. They would not raise their voices as if the patient were deaf. In short, they would treat the patient as a human being, not as a "diagnosis." If this sounds like a lot, it can all be done with a few sentences. The accompanying behaviors will do the rest.

Medical decision-making and care are all carried on at warp speed in today's world. There are productivity standards. Health insurance mandates the number of days paid for, unless an exception can be made, meaning extra paperwork. Patient care has suffered. The squeaky wheel gets the grease.

Or the insured do. This often results in quantity instead of quality. It's a complicated world for medical practice and it's a wonder that healing takes place in spite of it. And it's amazing that so many people go into the healing professions. Obviously, they do so from the heart.

One last note based on every emergency medical transport I've ever had! Ambulance drivers should keep in mind that the stretcher they are transporting may hold an aware, fearful person in pain, not an unconscious body. They should greet patients using their names in an unhurried, kind manner, making eye contact. They should tell them where they are going and about how long it will take. They should place the straps firmly around them and ask if they feel secure. One attendant should stay beside the person, preferably with his hands on the stretcher, while the other drives. Under no circumstances should the two attendants be joking with each other, or showing concern about the condition of the road, or admitting to not knowing where they are going. The driver should never take his eyes off the road to turn and talk to his buddy. I experienced every one of the mistakes above and was terrified every minute. And it was unnecessary.

SIXTH, participate in your family member's therapy. Ask medical personnel how you can be supportive. With cognitively compromised patients, it will help if family members can bring in pictures labeled with names and relationships. Not only can they share these with the patient, but occupational therapists will find this useful in orienting and helping patients regain their memories.

SEVENTH, medical personnel broke patient confidentiality in every medical setting I was in, talking about other patients in my presence. It seriously undermined my confidence in their professionalism. I know for a fact that the importance of confidentiality is drilled into medical personnel at every level. This is an offense that can affect a medical facility's credentials negatively as well as result in legal prosecution or firing.

EIGHTH, trust your own instincts. You know your own body and mind. Instinct is a powerful force in each of us. Many of us ignore what it tells us, listening to others' opinions. It's something so important to your welfare that you should never ignore it. You can use it to raise questions and even do research on your own through medical sites. Listening to my own instincts, I was able to think positively and question my diagnosis. And others spoke of their instincts about me which made me hopeful. I'm a strong believer in them!

NINTH, believe that prayer can work for you. Ask others to pray and do so yourself. There were many who prayed for me, and I thank God for each of you. I believe God heard you. Medical personnel know prayers are a powerful force which have been known to work miracles. If something terrible happens in your life, don't despair. Put your faith in God, the source of our strength.

Start each day with prayers of gratitude. My experiences over the five years covered in this memoire have brought many job changes in my life including counselor. A sequence of negative events ended up with positive results. Doors closed, windows opened.

Made in the USA
Columbia, SC
19 February 2022

56500385R00083